Probabilit
An aid to F

Martin Farquhar Tupper

Alpha Editions

This edition published in 2024

ISBN 9789362516701

Design and Setting By
Alpha Editions
www.alphaedis.com
Email - info@alphaedis.com

As per information held with us this book is in Public Domain.
This book is a reproduction of an important historical work.
Alpha Editions uses the best technology to reproduce historical work
in the same manner it was first published to preserve its original nature.
Any marks or number seen are left intentionally to preserve.

Contents

AN AID TO FAITH.	- 1 -
A GOD: AND HIS ATTRIBUTES.	- 8 -
THE TRIUNITY.	- 13 -
THE GODHEAD VISIBLE.	- 17 -
THE ORIGIN OF EVIL.	- 21 -
COSMOGONY.	- 26 -
ADAM.	- 29 -
THE FALL.	- 31 -
THE FLOOD.	- 34 -
NOAH.	- 36 -
BABEL.	- 39 -
JOB.	- 41 -
JOSHUA.	- 46 -
THE INCARNATION.	- 48 -
MAHOMETANISM.	- 51 -
ROMANISM.	- 53 -
THE BIBLE.	- 59 -
HEAVEN AND HELL.	- 63 -
AN OFFER.	- 67 -
CONCLUSION.	- 69 -

AN AID TO FAITH.

THE certainty of those things which most surely are believed among us, is a matter quite distinct from their antecedent probability or improbability. We know, and take for facts, that Cromwell and Napoleon existed, and are persuaded that their characters and lives were such as history reports them: but it is another thing, and one eminently calculated to disturb any disbeliever of such history, if a man were enabled to show, that, from the condition of social anarchy, there was an antecedent likelihood for the use of military despots; that, from the condition of a popular puritanism, or a popular infidelity, it was previously to have been expected that such leaders should have the several characteristics of a bigoted zeal for religion, or a craving appetite for worldly glory; that, from the condition liable to revolutions, it was probable to find such despots arising out of the middle class; and that, from the condition of reaction incidental to all human violences, there was a clear expectability that the power of such military monarchs should not be continued to their natural heirs.

Such a line of argument, although in no measure required for the corroboration of facts, might have considerable power to persuade *à priori* the man, who had not hitherto seen reason to credit such facts from posterior evidence. It would have rolled away a great stone, which to such a mind might otherwise have stood as a stumbling-block on the very threshold of truth. It would have cleared off a heavy mist, which might prevent him from discerning the real nature of the scene in which he stood. It would have shown him that, what others know to be fact, is, even to him who does not know it, become antecedently probable; and that Reason is not only no enemy to Faith, but is ready and willing to acknowledge its alliance.

Take a second illustration, by way of preliminary. A woodman, cleaving an oak, finds an iron ball in its centre; he sees the fact, and of course believes; some others believing on his testimony. But a certain village-pundit, habitually sceptical of all marvels, is persuaded that the wonder has been fabricated by our honest woodman; until the parson, a good historian, coming round that way, proclaims it a most interesting circumstance, because it was one naturally to have been expected; for that, here was the spot where, two hundred years ago, a great battle had been fought: and it was no improbability at all that a carbine-bullet should have penetrated a sapling, nor that the tree should thereafter have grown old with the iron at its heart. How unreasonable then would appear the pundit's incredulity, if persisted in: how suddenly enlightened the rational faith of the rustic: how seasonable would be felt the useful learning of him, whose knowledge well applied can thus unfetter truth from the bandages of ignorance.

Illustrations, if apt, are so well adapted to persuade towards a particular line of argument, that, at the risk of diffuseness, and because minds being various are variously touched, one by one thought and one by another, I think fit to add yet more of a similar tendency: in the hope that, by a natural induction, such instances may smoothe our way.

When an eminent living geologist was prosecuting his researches at Kirkdale cave, Yorkshire, he had calculated so nicely on the antecedent probabilities, that his commands to the labourers were substantially these: "Take your mattocks, and pick up that stone flooring; then take your basket, and fill it—with the bones of hyænas and other creatures which you will find there." We may fancy the ridicule wherewith ignorance might have greeted science: but lo, the triumph of philosophy, when its mandate soon assumed a bodily shape in—bushels of bones gnawed as by wild beasts, and here and there a grinning skull that looked like a hyæna's! Do we not see how this bears on our coming argument? Such a deposit was very unlikely to be found there in the eyes of the unenlightened: but very likely to the wise man's ken. The real probabilities were in favour of a strange fact, though the seeming probabilities were against it.

Take another. We are all now convinced of the existence of America; and so, some three or four hundred years back, was Christopher Columbus—but nobody else. Alone, he proved that mighty continent so probable, from geometrical measurements, and the balance of the world, and tides, and trade-winds, and casual floatsams driven from some land beneath the setting sun, that he was antecedently convinced of the fact: and it would have been a shock to his reason, as well as to his faith, had he found himself able to sail due west from Lisbon to China, without having struck against his huge probability. I purposely abstain from applying every illustration, or showing its specific difference regarding our theme. It is better to lead a mind to think for itself than to endeavour to forestall every notion.

Another. A Kissoor merchant in Timbuctoo is told of the existence of water hard and cold as marble. All the experience of his nation is against it. He disbelieves. However, after no long time, the testimony of two native princes who have been *fêted* in England, and have seen ice, shakes his once not unreasonable incredulity: and the additional idea brought soon to his remembrance, that, as lead cools down from hot fluidity to a solid lump, so, in the absence of solar heat, in all probability would water—corroborates and makes acceptable by analogous likelihood the doctrine simultaneously evidenced by credible witnesses.

Yet one more illustration for the last. Few things in nature appear more unlikely to the illiterate, than that a living toad should be found prisoned in a block of limestone; nevertheless, evidence goes to prove that such cases are not uncommon. Now, if, instead of limestone, which is a water-product, the creature had been found embedded in granite, which is a fire-product; although the fact might have been from eye-sight equally unimpeachable, how much more unlikely such a circumstance would have appeared in the judgment of science. To the rustic, the limestone case is as stout a puzzle as the granite one; but *à priori*, the philosopher—taking into account the aqueous fluidity of such a matrix at a period when reptiles were abundant, the torpid qualities of the toad itself, and the fact that time is scarcely an element in the absence of air—arrives at an antecedent probability, which comforts his acceptance of the fact. The granite would have staggered his reason, even though his own experience or the testimony of others were sufficient, nay, imperative, to assure his faith: but in the case of limestone, Reason even helps Faith; nay, anticipates and leads it in, by suggesting the wonder to be previously probable. How truly, and how strongly this bears upon our theme, let any such philosophizing mind consider.

But enough of illustrations: although these, multipliable to any amount, might bring, each in its own case, some specific tendency to throw light upon the path we mean to tread: it is wiser perhaps, as implying more confidence in the reader's intellectual powers, to leave other analogous cases to the suggestion of his own mind; also, not to vex him in every instance with the intrusive finger of an obvious application. Meanwhile, it is a just opportunity to clear the way at once of some obstructions, by disposing of a few matters personal to the writer; and by touching upon sundry other preliminary considerations.

1. The line of thought proposed is intended to show it probable that any thing which has been or is, might, viewed antecedently to its existence, by an exercise of pure reason, have by possibility been guessed: and on the hypothesis of sufficient keenness and experience, that this idea may be carried even to the future. Any thing, meaning every thing, is a word not used unadvisedly; for this is merely a suggestive treatise, starting a rule capable of infinite application: and, notwithstanding that we have here and now confined its elucidation to some matters of religious moment only, as occupying a priority of importance, and at all times deserving the lead; still, if knowledge availed, and time and space permitted, I scarcely doubt that a vigorous and illuminated intellect might so far enlarge on the idea, as to show the antecedent probability of every event which has happened in the

kingdoms of nature, providence, and grace: nay, of directing his guess at coming matters with no uncertain aim into the realms of the immediate future. The perception of cause in operation enables him to calculate the consequence, even perhaps better than the prophecy of cause could in the prior case enable him to suspect the consequence. But, in this brief life, and under its disturbing circumstances, there is little likelihood of accomplishing in practice all that the swift mind sees it easy to dream in theory: and if other and wiser pens are at all helped in the good aim to justify the ways of God with man, and to clear the course of truth, by some of the notions broadcast in this treatise, its errand will be well fulfilled.

2. Whether or not the leading idea, so propounded, is new, or is new in its application as an auxiliary to Christian evidences, the writer is unaware: to his own mind it has occurred quite spontaneously and on a sudden; neither has he scrupled to place it before others with whatever ill advantage of celerity, because it seemed to his own musings to shed a flood of light upon deep truths, which may not prove unwelcome nor unuseful to the doubting minds of many. It is true that in this, as in most other human efforts, the realization of idea in concrete falls far short of its abstract conception in the mind: there, all was clear, quick, and easy; here, the necessity of words, and the constraints of an unwilling perseverance, clog alike the wings of fancy and the feet of sober argument: insomuch that the difference is felt to be quite humiliating between the thoughts as they were thought, and the thoughts as they are written. Minerva, springing from the head of Jove, is not more unlike the heavily-treading Vulcan.

3. Necessarily, that the argument be (so to speak) complete, and on the wise principle that no fortresses be left untaken in the rear, it must be the writer's fate to attempt a demonstration of the anterior probability of truths, which a child of reason can not only now never doubt as fact, but never could have thought improbable. Instance the first effort, showing it to have been expectable that there should, in any conceived beginning, have existed a Something, a Great Spirit, whom we call God. To have to argue of the mighty Maker, that HE was an antecedent probability, would appear a most needless attempt; if it did not occur as the first link in a chain of arguments less open to objection by the thoughtless. With our little light to try to prove *à priori* the dazzling mystery of a Divine Tri-unity, might (unreasonably viewed) be assailed as a presumptuous and harmful thing; but it is our wise prerogative, if and when we can, to "Prove all things." Moreover, we live in a world wherein Truth's greatest enemy is the man who shrinks from endeavouring at least to clear away the mists and clouds that veil her precious aspect; and at a time when it behooves the reverent Christian to put on his panoply of faith and prayer, and meet in argument, according to the grace and power given to him—not indeed the

blaspheming infidel, for such a foe is unreasonable and unworthy of an answer, but—the often candid, anxious, and involuntary doubter; the mind, which, righteously vexed with the thousand corruptions of truth, and sorely disappointed at the conduct of its herd of false disciples, from a generous misconception is embracing error: the mind, never enough tenderly treated, but commonly taunted as a sceptic which yet with a natural manliness asserts the just prerogative of thinking for itself: fairly enough requiring, though rarely finding, evidence either to prop the weakness of a merely educational faith, or to argue away the objections to Christianity so rife in the clashing doctrines and unholy lives of its pseudo-sectaries. One of our poets hath said, "He has no hope who never had a fear:" it is quite as true (and take this saying for thy comfort, any harassed misbelieving mind), He has no faith, who never had a doubt. There is hope of a mind which doubts, because it thinks; because it troubles itself to think about what the mass of nominal Christians live threescore years and die of very mammonism, without having had one earnest thought about one difficulty, or one misgiving: there is hope of a man, who, not licentious nor scornful, from simple misconception, misbelieves; there is just and reasonable hope that (the misconception once removed) his faith will shine forth all the warmer for a temporary state of winter. To such do I address myself: not presumptuously imagining that I can satisfy by my poor thoughts all the doubts, cavils and objections of minds so keen and curious; not affecting to sail well among the shoals of metaphysics, nor to plumb unerringly the deeper gulphs of reason; but asking them for awhile to bear with me and hear me to the end patiently; with me, convinced of what (κατ' εξοχὴν) is Truth, by far surer and stronger arguments than any of the less considerations here expounded as auxiliary thereto; to bear with me, and prove for themselves at this penning of my thoughts (if haply I am helped in such high enterprise), whether indeed those doctrines and histories which the Christian world admit, were antecedently improbable, that is, unreasonable: whether, on the contrary, there did not exist, prior to any manifestation of such facts and doctrines, an exceeding likelihood that they would be so and so developed: and whether on the whole, led by reason to the threshold of faith, it may be worth while to encounter other arguments, which have rendered probabilities now certain.

4. It is very material to keep in memory the only scope and object of this essay. We do not pretend to add one jot of evidence, but only to prepare the mind to receive evidence: we do not attempt to prove facts, but only to accelerate their admission by the removal of prejudice. If a bed-ridden meteorologist is told that it rains, he may or he may not receive the fact from the force of testimony; but he will certainly be more prëdisposed to receive it, if he finds that his weatherglass is falling rather than rising. The fact remains the same, it rains; but the mind—precluded by circumstances

from positive personal assurance of such fact, and able only to arrive at truth from exterior evidence—is in a fitter state for belief of the fact from being already made aware that it was probable. Let it not then be inferred, somewhat perversely, that because antecedent probabilities are the staple of our present argument, the theme itself, Religion, rests upon hypotheses so slender: it rests not at all upon such straws as probabilities, but on posterior evidence far more firm. What we now attempt is not to prop the ark, but favourably to prëdispose the mind of any reckless Uzzah, who might otherwise assail it; not to strengthen the weak places of religion, but to annul such disinclination to receive Truth, as consists in prejudice and misconception of its likelihood. The goodly ship is built upon the stocks, the platforms are reared, and the cradle is ready; but mistaken prëconceptions may scatter the incline with gravel-stones rather than with grease, and thus put a needless hindrance to the launching: whereas a clear idea that the probabilities are in favour, rather than the reverse, will make all smooth, lubricate, and easy. If, then, we fail in this attempt, no disservice whatever is done to Truth itself; no breach is made in the walls, no mine sprung, no battlement dismantled; all the evidences remain as they were; we have taken nothing away. Even granting matters seemed anteriorily improbable, still, if evidence proved them true, such anterior unlikelihood would entirely be merged in the stoutly proven facts. Moreover, if we be adjudged to have succeeded, we have added nothing to Truth itself; no, nor to its outworks. That sacred temple stands complete, firm and glorious from corner-stone to top-stone. We do but sweep away the rubbish at its base; the drifting desert sands that choke its portals. We only serve that cause (a most high privilege), by enlisting a prëjudgment in its favour. We propose herein an auxiliary to evidence, not evidence itself; a finger-post to point the way to faith; a little light of reason on its path. The risk is really nothing; but the advantage, under favour, may be much.

5. It is impossible to elude the discussion of topics, which in their direct tendencies, or remoter inferences, may, to the author at least, prove dangerous or disputable ground. If a "great door and effectual" is opened to him, doubtless he will raise or meet with many adversaries. Besides mere haters of his creed, despisers of his arguments, and protestors, loud and fierce against his errors; he may possibly fall foul of divers unintended heresies; he may stumble unwittingly on the relics of exploded schisms; he may exhume controversies in metaphysical or scholastical polemics, long and worthily extinct. If this be so, he can only plead, *Mea culpa, mea culpa, mea maxima culpa.* But it is open to him also to protest against the common critical folly of making an offender for a word: of driving analogies on all four feet, and straining thoughts beyond their due proportions. Above all, never let a reader stir one inch beyond, far less against, his own judgment: if there seem to be sufficient reasons, well: if otherwise, let me walk

uncompanied. The first step especially is felt to be a very difficult one; perhaps very debatable: for aught I know, it may be merely a vain insect caught in the cobweb of metaphysics, soon to be destroyed, and easily to be discussed at leisure by some Aranean logician. However, it seemed to my midnight musings a probable mode of arriving at truth, though somewhat unsatisfactorily told from poverty of thought and language. Moreover, it would have been, in such *à priori* argument, ridiculous to have commenced by announcing a posterior conclusion: for this cause did I do my humble best to work it out anew: and however supererogatory it may seem at first sight to the majority of readers, those keener minds whom I mainly address, and whose interests I wish to serve, will recognise the attempt as at least consistent: and will be ready to admit that if the arduous effort prove anteriorly a First Great Cause, and His attributes, be futile (which, however, I do not admit), it was an attempt unneeded on the score of its own merits; albeit, with an obvious somewhat of justice, pure reason may desire to begin at the beginning. No one, who thinks at all upon religion, however misbelieving, can entertain any mental prejudice against the existence of a Deity, or against the received character of His attributes. Such a man would be merely in a savage state, irrational: whilst his own mind, so speculating, would stand itself proof positive of an Intellectual Father; either immediately, as in the first man's case, or mediately, as in our own, it must have sprung out of that Being, who is emphatically the Good One—God. But if, as is possible, a mind, capable of thinking, and keen to think on other themes, from any cause, educational or moral, has neglected this great track of mediation, has "forgotten God," and "had him *not* in all his thoughts," such an one I invite to walk with me; and, in spite of all incompleteness and insufficiency, uncaptious of much that may haply be fanciful or false, briefly and in outline to test with me sundry probabilities of the Christian scheme, considered antecedently to its elucidation.

A GOD: AND HIS ATTRIBUTES.

I WILL commence with a noble, and, as I believe, an inspired sentence: than which no truth uttered by philosophers ever was more clearly or more sublimely expressed. "In the beginning was the Word: and the Word was with God; and the Word was God." In its due course, we will consider especially the difference between the Word and God; likewise the seeming contradiction, but true concord, of being simultaneously God, and with God. At present, and previously to the true commencement of our *à priori* thoughts, let us, by a word or two, paraphrase that brief but comprehensive sentence, "In the beginning was the Word." Eternity has no beginning, as it has no end: the clock of Time is futile there: it might as well attempt to go in vacuo. Nevertheless, in respect to finite intelligences like ourselves, seeing that eternity is an idea totally inconceivable, it is wise, nay it is only possible, to be presented to the mind piecemeal. Even our deepest mathematicians do not scruple to speak of points "infinitely remote;" as if in that phrase there existed no contradiction of terms. So, also, we pretend in our emptiness to talk of eternity past, time present, and eternity to come; the fact being that, muse as a man may, he can entertain no idea of an existence which is not measurable by time: any more than he can conceive of a colour unconnected with the rainbow, or of a musical note beyond the seven sounds. The plain intention of the words is this: place the starting-post of human thought as far back into eternity as you will, be it what man counts a thousand ages, or ten thousand times ten thousand, or be these myriads multiplied again by millions, still, in any such Beginning, and in the beginning of all beginnings (for so must creatures talk)—then was God. He Was: the scholar knows full well the force of the original term, the philological distinctions between ειμι and γιγνομαι: well pleased, he reads as of the Divinity ἠν, He self-existed; and equally well pleased he reads of the humanity ἐγεννήθη, he was born. The thought and phrase ἠν sympathizes, if it has not an identity, with the Hebrew's unutterable Name. HE then, whose title, amongst all others likewise denoting excellence supreme and glory underivative, is essentially "I am;" HE who, relatively to us as to all creation else, has a new name wisely chosen in "the Word,"—the great expression of the idea of God; this mighty Intelligence is found in any such beginning self-existent. That teaching is a mere fact, known posteriorly from the proof of all things created, as well as by many wonderful signs, and the clear voice of revelation. We do not attempt to prove it; that were easy and obvious: but our more difficult endeavour at present is to show how antecedently probable it was that God should be: and that so being,

He should be invested with the reasonable attributes, wherewithal we know His glorious Nature to be clothed.

Take then our beginning where we will, there must have existed in that "originally" either Something, or Nothing. It is a clear matter to prove, *à posteriori*, that Something did exist; because something exists now: every matter and every derived spirit must have had a Father; *ex nihilo nihil fit*, is not more a truth, than that creation must have had a Creator. However, leaving this plain path (which I only point at by the way for obvious mental uses), let us now try to get at the great antecedent probability that in the beginning Something should have been, rather than Nothing.

The term, Nothing, is a fallacious one: it does not denote an existence, as Something does, but the end of an existence. It is in fact a negation, which must presuppose a matter once in being and possible to be denied; it is an abstraction, which cannot happen unless there be somewhat to be taken away; the idea of vacuity must be posterior to that of fullness; the idea of no tree is incompetent to be conceived without the previous idea of *a* tree; the idea of nonentity suggests, *ex vi termini*, a pre-existent entity; the idea of Nothing, of necessity, presupposes Something. And a Something once having been, it would still and for ever continue to be, unless sufficient cause be found for its removal; that cause itself, you will observe, being a Something. The chances are forcibly in favour of continuance, that is of perpetuity; and the likelihoods proclaim loudly that there should be an Existence. It was thus, then, antecedently more probable, than in any imaginable beginning from which reason can start, Something should be found existent, rather than Nothing. This is the first probability.

Next; of what nature and extent is this Something, this Being, likely to be?—There will be either one such being, or many: if many, the many either sprang from the one, or the mass are all self-existent; in the former case, there would be a creation and a God: in the latter, there would be many Gods. Is the latter antecedently more probable?—let us see. First, it is evident that if many are probable, few are more probable, and one most probable of all. The more possible gods you take away, the more do impediments diminish; until, that is to say, you arrive at that One Being, whom we have already proved probable. Moreover, many must be absolutely united as one; in which case the many is a gratuitous difficulty, because they may as well be regarded for all purposes of worship or argument as one God: or the many must have been in essence more or less disunited; in which case, as a state of any thing short of pure concord carries in itself the seeds of dissolution, needs must that one or other of the many (long before any possible beginnings, as we count beginnings, looking down the past vista of eternity), would have taken opportunity by such disturbing causes to become absolute monarch: whether by peaceful persuasion, or hostile compulsion, or other mode of absorbing disunions, would be indifferent; if they were not all improbable, as unworthy of the God. Perpetuity of discord is a thing impossible; every thing short of unity tends to decomposition. Any how then, given the element of eternity to work in, a one great Supreme Being was, in the created beginning, an *à priori* probability. That all other assumptions than that of His true and eternal Oneness are as false in themselves as they are derogatory to the rational views of deity, we all now see and believe; but the direct proofs of this are more strictly matters of revelation than of reason: albeit reason too can discern their probabilities. Wise heathens, such as Socrates and Cicero, who had not our light, arrived nevertheless at some of this perception; and thus, through conscience and intelligence, became a law unto themselves: because that, to them, as now to any one of us who may not yet have seen the light, the anterior likelihood existed for only one God, rather than more; a likelihood which prepares the mind to take as a fundamental truth, "The Lord our God is one Jehovah."

Next; Self-existence combined with unity must include the probable attribute, or character, Ubiquity; as I now proceed to show. On the same principle as that by which we have seen Something to be likelier than Nothing, we conclude that the same Something is more probable to be every where, than the same Nothing (if the phrase were not absurd), to be any where: we may, so to speak, divide infinity into spaces, and prove the position in each instance: moreover, as that Something is essentially—not a unit as of many, but—unity involving all, it follows as most probable that this Whole Being should be ubiquitous; in other parlance, that the one God should be every where at once: also, there being no limit to what we call Space, nor any imaginable hostile power to place a constraint upon the One Great Being, this Whole Being must be ubiquitous to a degree strictly infinite: "HE is in every place, beholding the evil and the good."

Such a consideration (and it is a perfectly true one) renders necessary the next point, to wit, that God is a Spirit. No possible substance can be every where at once: essence may, but not substance. Corporeity in any shape must be local; local is finite; and we have just proved the anterior probability of a One great Existence being (notwithstanding unity of essence) infinite. Illocal and infinite are convertible terms: spirit is illocal; and, as God is infinite—that is, illocal—it is clear that "God is a Spirit."

We have thus (not attempting to build up faith by such slight tools, but only using them to cut away prejudice) arrived at the high probability of a God invested with His natural qualities or attributes; Self-existence, Unity, the faculty of being every where at once and that every where Infinitude; and essentially of a Spiritual nature, not material. His moral, or accidental attributes (so to speak), were, antecedently to their expression, equally easy of being proved probable. First, with respect to Power: given no disturbing cause—(we shall soon consider the question of permitted evil, and its origin; but this, however disturbing to creatures, will be found not only none to God, but, as it were, only a ray of His glory suffered to be broken for prismatic beauty's sake, a flash of the direction of His energies suffered to be diverted for the superior triumph of good in that day when it shall be shown that "God hath made all things for himself, yea, even the wicked for the time of visitation")—with the *datum* then of no disturbing cause obstructing or opposing, an infinite being must be able to do all things within the sphere of such infinity: in other phrase, He must be all-powerful. Just so, an impetus in vacuity suffers no check, but ever sails along among the fleet of worlds; and the innate Impulse of the Deity must expand and energize throughout that infinitude, Himself. For a like reason of ubiquity, God must know all things: it is impossible to escape from the strong likelihood that any intelligent being must be conversant of what is going on under his very eye. Again; in the case both of Power and Knowledge, alike with the coming attributes of Goodness and Wisdom—(wisdom considered as morally distinct from mere knowledge or awareness; it being quite possible to conceive a cold eye seeing all things heedlessly, and a clear mind knowing all things heartlessly)—in the case, I say, of all these accidental attributes, there recurs for argument, one analogous to that by which we showed the anterior probability of a self-existence. Things positive must precede things negative. Sight must have been, before blindness is possible; and before we can arrive at a just idea of no sight. Power must be precursor to an abstraction from power, or weakness. The minor-existence of ignorance is an impossibility, unless you preällow the major-existence of wisdom; for it amounts to a debasing or a diminution of wisdom. Sin is well defined to be, the transgression of law; for without law, there can be no sin. So, also, without wisdom, there can be no ignorance; without power, there can be no weakness; without goodness, there can be no evil.

Furthermore. An affirmative—such as wisdom, power, goodness—can exist absolutely; it is in the nature of a Something: but a negative—such as ignorance, weakness, evil—can only exist relatively; and it would, indeed, be a Nothing, were it not for the previous and now simultaneous existence of its wiser, stronger, and better origin. Abstract evil is as demonstrably an impossibility as abstract ignorance, or abstract weakness. If evil could have self-existed, it would in the moment of its eternal birth have demolished itself. Virtue's intrinsic concord tends to perpetual being: vice's innate discord struggles always with a force towards dissolution. Goodness, wisdom, power have existences, and have had existences from all eternity, though gulphed within the Godhead; and that, whether evidenced in act or not: but their corruptions have had no such original existence, but are only the same entities perverted. Love would be love still, though there were no existent object for its exercise: Beauty would be beauty still, though there were no created thing to illustrate its fairness: Power would be power still, though there be no foe to combat, no difficulty to be overcome. Hatred, ill-favour, weakness, are only perversions or diminutions of these. Power exists independently of muscles or swords or screws or levers; love, independently of kind thoughts, words, and actions; beauty, independently of colours, shapes, and adaptations. Just so is Wisdom philosophically spoken of by a truly royal and noble author:

"I, wisdom, dwell with prudence, and find out the knowledge of clever inventions. Counsel is mine, and sound wisdom; I am understanding; I have strength. The Lord possessed me in the beginning of his way, before his works of old. I was set up from everlasting, from the beginning, or ever the earth was. When there were no depths, I was brought forth; before the mountains were fixed, or the hills were made. When He prepared the heavens, I was there; when he set a compass upon the face of the depth; when he established the clouds above; when he strengthened the foundations of the deep: Then was I by him, as one brought up with him: and I was daily his delight, rejoicing always before him; rejoicing in the habitable parts of his earth; and my delights were with the sons of men."

King Solomon well knew of Whom he wrote thus nobly. Eternal wisdom, power, and goodness, all prospectively thus yearning upon man, and incorporate in One, whose name, among his many names, is Wisdom. Wisdom, as a quality, existed with God; and, constituting full pervasion of his essence, was God.

But to return, and bind to a conclusion our ravelled thoughts. As, originally, the self-existent being, unbounded, all-knowing, might take up, so to speak, if He willed, these eternal affirmative excellences of wisdom, power, and goodness; and as these, to every rational apprehension, are highly worthy of his choice, whereas their derivative and inferior corruptions would have been most derogatory to any reasonable estimate of His character; how much more likely was it that He should prefer the higher rather than the lower, should take the affirmative before the negative, should "choose the good, and refuse the evil,"—than endure to be endowed with such garbled, demoralizing, finite attributes as those wherewith the heathen painted the Pantheon. What high antecedent probability was there, that if a God should be (and this we have proved highly probable too)—He should be One, ubiquitous, self-existent, spiritual: that He should be all-mighty, all-wise, and all-good?

THE TRIUNITY.

ANOTHER deep and inscrutable topic is now to engage our thoughts—the mystery of a probable Triunity. While we touch on such high themes, the Christian's presumption ever is, that he himself approaches them with reverence and prayer; and that, in the case of an unbeliever, any such mind will be courteous enough to his friendly opponent, and wise enough respecting his own interest and safety lest these things be true, to enter upon all such subjects with the seriousness befitting their importance, and with the restraining thought that in fact they may be sacred.

Let us then consider, antecedently to all experience, with what sort of deity pure reason would have been satisfied. It has already arrived at Unity, and the foregoing attributes. But what kind of Unity is probable? Unity of Person, or unity of Essence? A sterile solitariness, easily understandable, and presumably incommunicative? or an absolute oneness, which yet relatively involves several mysterious phases of its own expansive love? Will you think it a foregone conclusion, if I assert the superior likelihoods of the latter, and not of the former? Let us come then to a few of many reasons. First: it was by no means probable to be supposed anteriorly, that the God should be clearly comprehensible: yet he must be one: and oneness is the idea most easily apprehended of all possible ideas. The meanest of intellectual creatures could comprehend his Maker, and in so far top his heights, if God, being truly one in one view, were yet only one in every view: if, that is to say, there existed no mystery incidental to his nature: nay, if that mystery did not amount to the difficulty of a seeming contradiction. I judge it likely, and with confidence, that Reason would prërequire for his God, a Being, at once infinitely easy to be apprehended by the lowest of His spiritual children, and infinitely difficult to be comprehended by the highest of His seraphim. Now, there can be guessed only two ways of compassing such a prërequirement: one, a moral way; such as inventing a deity who could be at once just and unjust, every where and no where, good and evil, powerful and weak; this is the heathen phase of Numen's character, and is obviously most objectionable in every point of view: the other would be a physical way; such as requiring a God who should be at once material and immaterial, abstraction and concretion; or, for a still more confounding paradox to Reason (considered as antagonist to Faith, in lieu of being strictly its ally), an arithmetical contradiction, an algebraic mystery, such as would be included in the idea of Composite Unity; one involving many, and many collapsed into one. Some such enigma was probable in Reason's guess at the nature of his God. It is the Christian way;

and one entirely unobjectionable: because it is the only insuperable difficulty as to His Nature which does not debase the notion of Divinity. But there are also other considerations.

For, secondly. The self-existent One is endowed, as we found probable, with abundant loving-kindness, goodness overflowing and perpetual. Is it reasonable to conceive that such a character could for a moment be satisfied with absolute solitariness? that infinite benevolence should, in any possible beginning, be discovered existent in a sort of selfish only-oneness? Such a supposition is, to the eye of even unenlightened Reason, so clearly a *reductio ad absurdum*, that men in all countries and ages have been driven to invent a plurality of Gods, for very society sake: and I know not but that they are anteriorly wiser and more rational than the man who believes in a Benevolent Existence eternally one, and no otherwise than one. Let me not be mistaken to imply that there was any likelihood of many cöexistent gods: that was a reasonable improbability, as we have already seen, perhaps a spiritual impossibility: but the anterior likelihood of which I speak goes to show, that in One God there should be more than one cöexistence: each, by arithmetical mystery, but not absurdity, pervading all, cöequals, each being God, and yet not three Gods, but one God. That there should be a rational difficulty here—or, rather, an irrational one—I have shown to be Reason's prërequirement: and if such a one as I, or any other creature, could now and here (ay, or any when or any where, in the heights of highest heaven, and the far-stretching distance of eternity) solve such intrinsic difficulty, it would demonstrably be one not worthy of its source, the wise design of God: it would prove that riddle read, which uncreate omniscience propounded for the baffling of the creature mind. No. It is far more reasonable, as well as far more reverent, to acquiesce in Mystery, as another attribute inseparable from the nature of the Godhead; than to quibble about numerical puzzles, and indulge unwisely in objections which it is the happy state of nobler intelligences than man on earth is, to look into with desire, and to exercise withal their keen and lofty minds.

But we have not yet done. Some further thoughts remain to be thrown out in the third place, as to the prëconceivable fitness or propriety of that Holy Union, which we call the trinity of Persons who constitute the Self-existent One. If God, being one in one sense, is yet likely to appear, humanly speaking, more than one in another sense; we have to inquire anteriorly of the probable nature of such other intimate Being or Beings: as also, whether such addition to essential oneness is likely itself to be more than one or only one. As to the former of these questions: if, according to the presumption of reason (and according also to what we have since learned from revelation; but there may be good policy in not dotting this book with chapter and verse)—if the Deity thus loved to multiply Himself; then He, to whom there can exist no beginning, must have so loved, so determined, and so done from all eternity. Now, any conceivable creation, however originated, must have had a beginning, place it as far back as you will. In any succession of numbers, however infinitely they may stretch, the commencement at least is a fixed point, one. But, this multiplication of Deity, this complex simplicity, this intricate easiness, this obvious paradox, this sub-division and con-addition of a One, must have taken place, so soon as ever eternal benevolence found itself alone; that is, in eternity, and not in any imaginable time. So then, the Being or Beings would probably not have been creative, but of the essence of Deity. Take also for an additional argument, that it is an idea which detracts from every just estimate of the infinite and all-wise God to suppose He should take creatures into his eternal counsels, or consort, so to speak, familiarly with other than the united sub-divisions, persons, and cöequals of Himself. It was reasonable to prëjudge that the everlasting companions of Benevolent God, should also be God. And thus, it appears antecedently probable that (what from the poverty of language we must call) the multiplication of the one God should not have been created beings; that is, should have been divine; a term, which includes, as of right, the attribution to each such Holy Person, of all the wondrous characteristics of the Godhead.

Again: as to the latter question; was it probable that such so-called sub-divisions should be two, or three, or how many? I do not think it will be wise to insist upon any such arithmetical curiosity as a perfect number; nor on such a toy as an equilateral triangle and its properties; nor on the peculiar aptitude for sub-division in every thing, to be discerned in a beginning, a middle, and an end; nor in the consideration that every fact had a cause, is a constancy, and produces a consequence: neither, to draw any inferences from the social maxim that for counsel, companionship, and conversation, the number three has some special fitness. Some other similar fancies, not altogether valueless, might be alluded to. It seems preferable, however, on so grand a theme, to attempt a deeper dive, and a higher flight. We would then, reverently as always, albeit equally as always with the free-born boldness of God's intellectual children, attempt to prëjudge how many, and with what distinctive marks, the holy beings into whom (ὡς ἔπος εἰπἐιν) God, for very Benevolence sake, pours out Essential Unity, were likely to be.

Let us consider what principles, as in the case of a forthcoming creation, would probably be found in action, to influence such creation's Author.

First of all, there would be Will, a will energized by love, disposing to create: a phase of Deity aptly and comprehensively typified to all minds by the name of a universal Father: this would be the primary impersonation of God. And is it not so?

Secondly: there would be (with especial reference to that idea of creation which doubtless at most remote beginnings occupied the Good One's contemplation), there would be next, I repeat, in remarkable adaptation to all such benevolent views, the great idea of principle, Obedience; conforming to a Father's righteous laws, acquiescing in his just will, and returning love for love: such a phase could not be better shadowed out to creatures than by an Eternal Son; the dutiful yet supreme, the subordinate yet cöequal, the amiable yet exalted Avatar of our God. This was probable to have been the second impersonation of Deity. And is it not so?

Thirdly: Springing from the conjoint ideas of the Father and the Son, and with similar prospection to such instantly creative universe, there would occur the grand idea of Generation; the mighty cöequal, pure, and quickening Impulse: aptly announced to men and angels as the Holy Spirit. This was to have been the third impersonation of Divinity. And is it not so?

Of all these—under illumination of the fore-known fact, I speak, in their aspect of anterior probability. With respect to more possible Persons, I at least cannot invent one. There is, to my reflection, neither need nor fitness for a fourth, or any further Principle. If another can, let him look well that he be not irrationally demolishing an attribute and setting it up as a principle. Obedience is not an attribute; nor Generation; nor Will: whilst the attribute of Love, pervading all, sets these only possible three Principles going together as One in a mysterious harmony. I would not be misunderstood; persons are not principles; but principles may be illustrated and incorporative in persons. Essential Love, working distinctively throughout the Three, unites them instinctively as One: even as the attribute Wisdom designs, and the attribute Power arranges all the scheme of Godhead.

And now I ask Reason, whether, prësupposing keenness, he might not have arrived by calculation of probabilities at the likelihood of these great doctrines: that the nature of God would be an apparent contradiction: that such contradiction should not be moral, but physical; or rather verging towards the metaphysical, as immaterial and more profound: that God, being One, should yet, in his great Love, marvellously have been companioned from eternity by Himself: and that such Holy and United Confraternity should be so wisely contrived as to serve for the bright unapproachable exemplar of love, obedience, and generation to all the future universe, such Triunity Itself existing uncreated.

THE GODHEAD VISIBLE.

WE have hitherto mused on the Divinity, as on Spirit invested with attributes: and this idea of His nature was enough for all requirements antecedently to a creation. At whatever beginning we may suppose such creation to have commenced, whether countless ages before our present κὸσμος, or only a sufficient time to have prepared the crust of earth; and to whatever extent we may imagine creation to have spread, whether in those remote periods originally to our system alone and at after eras to its accompanying stars and galaxies and firmaments; or at one and the same moment to have poured material existence over space to which our heavens are as nothing: whatever, and whenever, and wherever creation took place, it would appear to be probable that some one person of the Deity should, in a sort, become more or less concretely manifested; that is, in a greater or a minor degree to such created minds and senses visible. Moreover, for purposes at least of a concentrated worship of such creatures, that He should occasionally, or perhaps habitually, appear local. I mean, that the King of all spiritual potentates and the subordinate Excellencies of brighter worlds than ours, the Sovereign of those whom we call angels, should will to be better known to and more aptly conceived by such His admiring creatures, in some usual glorious form, and some wonted sacred place. Not that any should see God, as purely God; but, as God relatively to them, in the capacity of King, Creator, and the Object of all reasonable worship. It seems anteriorly probable that one at least of the Persons in the Godhead should for this purpose assume a visibility; and should hold His court of adoration in some central world, such as now we call indefinitely Heaven. That such probability did exist in the human forecast, as concerns a heaven and the form of God, let the testimony of all nations now be admitted to corroborate. Every shape from a cloud to a crocodile, and every place from Æther to Tartarus, have been peopled by man's not quite irrational device with their so-called gods. But we must not lapse into the after-argument: previous likelihood is our harder theme. Neither, in this section, will we attempt the probabilities of the place of heaven: that will be found at a more distant page. We have here to speak of the antecedent credibility that there should be some visible phase of God; and of the shape wherein he would be most likely, as soon as a creation was, to appear to such his creatures. With respect, then, to the former. Creatures, being finite, can only comprehend the infinite in his attribute of unity: the other attributes being apprehended (or comprehended partially) in finite phases. But, unity being a purely intellectual thought, one high and dry beyond the moral feelings, involves none of the requisites of a spiritual, that is an affectionate, worship; such worship as it was likely that a beneficent Being would, for his creatures' own elevation in happiness, command and inspire towards Himself. In order, therefore, to such worship and such inspiration acting through reason, it would appear fitting that the Deity should manifest Himself especially with reference to that heavenly Exemplar, the Three Divine Persons of the One Supreme Essence already shown to have been probable. And it seems likeliest and discreetest to my thinking, that, with this view, the secondary phase, loving Obedience, under the dictate of the primary phase, a loving Will, and energized by the tertiary or conjoining phase a loving Quickening Entity, should assume the visible type of Godhead, and thus concentrate unto Himself the worship of all worlds. I can conceive no scheme more simply profound, more admirably suited to its complex purposes, than that He, in whom dwelt the fullness of the Godhead, bodily, should take the form of God, in order that unto Him every knee should bow, of things in heaven, and things in earth, and things in regions under the earth. Was not all this reasonably to have been looked for? and tested afterwards by Scripture, in its frequent allusions to some visible phase of Deity, when the Lord God walked with Adam, and Enoch, and Abraham, and Peter, and James, and John—I ask, is it not the case?

The latter point remaining to be thus briefly touched upon, respects the probable shape to be assumed and worn, familiarly enough to be recognised as His, by Deity thus vouchsafing Himself visible. And here we must look down the forward stream of Time, and search among the creatures whom thereafter God should make, to arrive at some good reason for, some antecedent probability of, the form which he should thus frequently inhabit. Fire, for example, a pure and spirit-like nature, would not have been a guess unworthy of reason: but this, besides its humbler economic uses, would endanger an idolatry of the natural emblem. So also would light be no irrational thought. And it is true that God might, and probably would, invest Himself in one or both of these pure essences, so seemingly congenial to a nature higher than ours: but then there would be some nucleus to the brilliancy and the burning; these would be as a veil to the Divinity; we should have need, before He were truly visible, that the veil were laid aside: we should have to shred away to the nucleus, which (and not the fire or light) would be the form of God. Similar objections, in themselves or in their idolatrizing tendencies, would lie against any such shape as a cloud, or a rainbow, or an angel (whatever such a being may resemble), or in fact any other conceivable creature, whether good as the angelic case or indifferent as that of the cloud, which the Deity, though assuming often, would nevertheless in every instance assume in conjunction with such his ordinary creature, and could not entirely monopolize. I mean; if God had the shape of a cloud, or of a rainbow, common clouds and rainbows would come to be thought gods too. Reason would anticipate this objection to such created and too-favoured shapes: more; in every case, but one, he would be quite at a loss to look for some type, clearly apt and probable. That one case he might discern to be this. Known unto God are all things from the beginning to the end: and, in His fore-knowledge, Reason might have been enlightened to prophesy (as we shall hereafter see) that for certain wise and good ends one great family out of the myriads who rejoice in being called God's children, would in a most marked manner fall away from Him through disobedience; and should thereby earn, if not the annihilation of their being, at least its endless separation from the Blessed. Manifestly, the wisdom and benevolence of God would be eager and swift to devise a plan for the redemption of so lost a race. Why He should permit their fall at all will be reverentially descanted on in its proper section; meanwhile, how is it probable that God, first, by any theory consistently with truth and justice, could, and next by power and contrivance actually would, lift up again this sinful family from the pit of condemnation? Reason is to search the question well: and after much thought, you will arrive at the truth that there was but one way probable. Rebellion against the Great and Self-existent Author of all things, must needfully involve infinite punishment; if only because He is infinite, and his laws of an eternal sanction. The problem then was, how to inflict the unbounded punishment thus claimed by justice for a transgressional condition, and yet at love's demand to set the prisoner free: how to be just, and simultaneously justifier of the guilty. That was a question magnificently solved by God alone: magnificently about to be solved, as according to our argument seemed probable, by God Triune, in wondrous self-involving council. The solution would be rationally this. Himself, in his character of filial obedience, should pay the utter penalty to Himself in his character of paternal authority, whilst Himself in the character of quickening spirit, should restore the ransomed family from death to life, from the power of evil unto good. Was not this a most probable, a most reasonably probable scheme? was it not altogether wise and philosophical, as well as entirely generous and kind to wretched men?

And (returning to our present topic), was it not antecedently to have been expected that God the Son (so to put it) should, in the shape He was thereafter to assume upon earth, appear upon the eternal throne of heaven? In a shape, however glorified and etherealized, with glistening countenance and raiment bright as the light, nevertheless resembling that more humble form, the Son of Man, who was afterwards thus by a circle of probabilities to be made in the form of God; in a shape, not liable, from its very sinfulness, to the deification either of other worlds or of this [hero-worship is another and a lower thing altogether; we speak here of true idolatries:]— was it unlikely, I say, that in such a shape Deity should have deigned to become visible, and have blazed Manifested God, the central Sun of Heaven?—This probability, prior to our forth-flowing thoughts on the Incarnation, though in some measure anticipating them, will receive further light from the views soon to be set forth. I know not but that something is additionally due to the suggestion following; namely: that, raise our swift imagination to what height we may, and stretch our searching reason to the uttermost, we cannot, despite of all inventive energies and powers of mind, conceive any shape more beautiful, more noble, more worthy for a rational intelligence to dwell in, more in one Homeric word Θεοειδές, than the glorified and etherealized human form divine. Let this serve as Reason's short reply to any charge of anthropomorphism in the doctrines of his creed: it was probable that God should be revealed to His creation; and as to the form of any such revealed essence in any such infinite beginnings of His work, the most likely of all would appear to be that one, wherein He, in the ages then to come, was well resolved to earn the most glorious of all triumphs, the merciful reconciliation of everlasting justice with everlasting love, the wise and wondrous scheme of God forgiving sinners.

THE ORIGIN OF EVIL.

IT will now be opportune to attempt elucidation of one of the darkest and deepest riddles ever propounded to the finite understanding; the *à priori* likelihood of evil: not, mind, its eternal existence, which is a false doctrine; but its probable procession from the earliest created beings, which is a true one.

At first sight, nothing could appear more improbable: nothing more inconsistent with the recognised attributes of God, than that error, pain, and sorrow should be mingled in His works. These, the spontaneous offspring of His love, one might (not all wisely) argue, must always be good and happy—because perfect as Himself. Because perfect?—Therein lies the fallacy, which reason will at once lay bare. Perfection is attributable to no possible creature: perfection argues infinity, and infinity is one of the prerogatives of God. However good, "very good," a creation may be found, still it must, from essential finitude, fall short of that Best, which is in effect the only state purely unexceptionable. For instance, no creature can be imagined of a wisdom undiminished from the single true standard, God's wisdom: in other phrase, every creature must be more or less departed from wisdom, that is, verging towards folly. Again; no creature can be presumed of a purity so spotless as to rank in an equality with that of the Almighty: in other words, neither man, nor angel, nor any other creature, can exist who is not more or less—I will not say impure, positively, but— unpure negatively. Thus, the birth-mark of creation must have been an inclination towards folly, and from purity. The mere idea of creatures would involve, as its great need-be, the qualifying clause that these emanations from perfection be imperfect; and that these children of purity be liable to grow unpure. They must either be thus natured, or exist of the essence of God, that is, be other persons and phases of the Deity: such a case was possible certainly; but, as we have already shown, not probable. And it were possible, that, in consequence of some redemption such as we have spoken of, creatures might by ingraftation into God become so entirely part of Him—bone of bone, and flesh of flesh, and spirit of spirit—that an exhortation to such blest beings should reasonably run, "Be ye perfect." But this infinite munificence of the Godhead in redemption was not to be found among His bounties as Creator. It might indeed arise afterwards, as setting up again the fallen creature in some safe niche of Deity: and we now know it has arisen: "we are complete in Him."

But this, though relevant, is a digression. Returning, and to produce some further argument against all creature perfectness; let us consider how rational it seems to presuppose that the mighty Maker in his boundless love should have willed to form a long chain of classes of existence more and more subordinated each to the other, each good of its kind and happy in its way, but yet all needfully more or less removed from the high standard of uncreate Perfection. These descending links, these graduations downwards, must involve a nearer or remoter approach to evil. Now, we must bear in mind that Evil is not a principle, but a perversion: it amounts merely to a denial, a limitation, a corruption of good, not to the dignity of its abstract antagonism. Familiarly, but fallaciously, we talk of the evil principle, the contradictory to good: we might as well talk of the nosologic principle, the contradictory to health; or the darkness principle, the contradictory to light. They are contraries, but not contradictories: they have no positive, but only a relative existence. Good and evil are verily foes, but originally there was one cemented friendship: slender beginnings consequent on a creation, began to cause the breach: the civil war arose out of a state of primitive peace: images betray us into errors, or I might add with a protest against the risk of being misinterpreted, that like brothers turned to a deadly hate, they nevertheless sprang not originally out of two hostile and opposite hemispheres, but from one paternal hearth. Not, however, in any sense that God is the author of evil; but that God's workmanship, the finite creature, needfully perverted good.

The origin of evil—that is, its birth—is a term true and clear: original evil—that is, giving it no birth but an antedate to all created things, suffering it to run parallel with God and good from all eternity—this is a term false and misty. The probability that good would be warped, and grow deteriorate; that wisdom would be dwindled down into less and less wisdom, or foolishness; and power degenerated more and more towards imbecility; must arise, directly a creature should spring out of the Creator; and that, let astronomy or geology name any date they will: Adam is a definite date; perhaps also the first day's—or period's—work: but the Beginning of Creation is undated. It would then, under this impression of the necessary defalcation of the creature from the strict straight line, be rational to look for deviations: it would be rational to presuppose that God—just, and good, and pure, and wise—should righteously be able to "charge his angels with folly," should verily declare that "the heavens are not pure in his sight."

Further; it would be a possible chance (which considerations soon succeeding would render even probable) that for a wise humiliation of the reasoning creature, and a just exaltation of the only Source of life and light and all things, one or more of such first created beings, or angels, should be suffered to fall, possibly from the vastest height, and at first by the slenderest beginnings, lower and lower into folly, impurity, and all other derelictions from the excellence of God. The lines, once unparalleled, would, without a check, go further apart for all eternity; albeit, the primal deviation arose in time. The aerolite, dropping slowly at first, increases in swiftness as it multiplies the fathoms of descent: and if the abyss be really bottomless, how impossible a check or a return.

Some such terrible example would amount to a reasonable likelihood, if only for a lesson and a warning: to all intelligent hierarchs, be not high-minded, but fear; to all responsible beings, keep righteousness and reverence, and tempt not God; to all the Virtues, Dominations, Obediences, and due Subordinations of unknown glorious worlds, a loud and living exhortation to exercise, and not to let grow dim their spiritual energies, in efforts after goodness, wisdom, and purity. A creature state, to be happy, must be a progressive state: the capability of progression argues lack, or a tendency from good: and progression itself needs a spur, lest indolence relapse towards evil.

Additionally: we must remember that a creature's excellence before God is the reasonable service which he freely renders: freedom, dangerous prerogative, involves choice: and choice necessitates the possibility of error. The command to a rational intelligence would be, do this, and live; do it not, and die: if thou doest, it is well done, good and faithful servant; thou hast mounted by thine own heaven-blest exertions to a higher approach towards infinite perfection; enter thou into the joy, not merely of a creature, but of thy Lord. But, if thou doest not, it is wo to thee, unworthy hireling; thou hast broken the tie that bound thee to thy Maker—obedience, the root of happiness; thou livest on indeed, because the Former of all things cancelleth not nor endeth his beginning; but henceforth thine existence is, as a river which earthquakes have divorced from its bed, and instead of flowing on for ever through the fair pastures of peace and among the mountain roots of everlasting righteousness, thy downward course is shattery, headlong, turbulent, and destructive; black-throated whirlpools here, miasmatic marshes there, a cataract, a shoal, a rapid; until the remorseless stream, lashing among rocks which its own riot rendered sterile, pours its unresting waters into the thirsty sands of the Sahara.

It was indeed probable (as since we know it to be true) that the generous Giver of all things would in the vast majority of cases minister such secret help to His weaker spiritual children, that, far from failing of continuous obedience, they should find it so unceasingly easier and happier that their very natures would soon come to be imbued with that pervading habit: and that thus, the longer any creature stood upright, the stronger should he rest in righteousness; until, at no very distant period, it should become morally impossible for him to fall. Such would soon be the condition of myriads, perhaps almost the whole, of heaven's innumerable host: and with respect to any darker Unit in that multitude, for the good of all permitted to make early shipwreck of himself, simply by leaving his intelligence to plume its wings into presumptuous flight, and by allowing his pristine goodness or wisdom to grow rusty from non-usage until that sacred panoply were eaten into holes; with respect to any such unhappy one, and all others (if others be) who should listen to his glozing, and make a common cause in his rebellion, where, I ask, is any injustice, or even unkindness done to him by Deity? Where is any moral improbability that such a traitor should be; or any just inconsistency chargeable on the attributes of God in consequence of such his being? Whom can he in reason accuse but himself for what he is? And what misery can such a one complain of, which is not the work of his own hands? And lest the Great Offender should urge against his God, why didst thou make me thus?—Is not the answer obvious, I made thee, but not thus. And on the rejoinder, Why didst thou not keep me as thou madest me? Is not the reply just, I made thee reasonable, I led thee to the starting place, I taught thee and set thee going well in the beginning; thou art intelligent and free, and hast capacities of Mine own giving: wherefore didst thou throw aside My grace, and fly in the face of thy Creator?

On the whole; consider that I speak only of probabilities. There is a depth in this abyss of thought, which no human plummet is long enough to sound; there is a maze in this labyrinth to be tracked by no mortal clue. It involves the truth, How unsearchable are his judgments: Thou hidest thy ways in the sea, and thy paths in the deep waters, and thy footsteps are not known. The weak point of man's argument lies in the suggested recollection, that doubtless the Deity could, if He would, have upheld all the universe from falling by his gracious power; and that the attribute of love concludes that so He would. However, these three brief considerations further will go some way to solve the difficulty, and to strengthen the weak point; first, there are other attributes besides love to run concurrently with it, as truth, justice, and unchangeableness:—Secondly, that grace is not grace, if manifested indiscriminately to all: and thirdly, that to our understanding at least there was no possible method of illustrating the amiabilities of Goodness, and the contrivances of Wisdom, but by the infused permission of some physical and moral evils: Mercy, benevolence, design, would in a universe of best have nothing to do; that universe itself would grow stagnant, as incapable of progress; and the principal record of God's excellences, the book of redemption, would have been unwritten. Is not then the existence of evil justified in reason's calculation? and was not such existence an antecedent probability?

Of these matters, thus curtly: it is time, in a short recapitulation, to reflect, that, from foregoing causes, mysteries were probable around the throne of heaven: and, as I have attempted to show, the mystery of imperfection, a concrete not an abstract, was likely to have sprung out of any creature universe. Reason perceives that a Gordion knot was likely to have become entangled; in the intricate complexities of abounding good to be mingled needfully with its own deficiencies, corruptions, and perversions: and this having been shown by Reason as anteriorly probable, its difficult involvements are now since cut by the sword of conquering Faith.

COSMOGONY.

THESE deep themes having been descanted on, however from their nature unsatisfactorily and with whatever human weakness, let us now endeavour mentally to transport ourselves to a period immediately antecedent to our own world's birth. We should then have been made aware that a great event was about to take place; whereat, from its foreseen consequences, the hierarchies of heaven would be prompt to shout for joy, and the holy ones of God to sing for gratitude. It was no common case of a creation; no merely onemore orb, of third-rate unimportance, amongst the million others of higher and more glorious praise: but it was a globe and a race about to be unique in character and fate, and in the far-spread results of their existence. On it and of its family was to be contrived the scene, wherein, to the admiration of the universe, God himself in Person was going visibly to make head against corruption in creation, and for ever thus to quench that possibility again: wherein He was marvellously to invent and demonstrate how Mercy and Truth should meet together, how Righteousness and Peace should kiss each other. There, was going to be set forth the wonderfully complicated battle-plan, by which, force countervailing force, and design converging all things upon one fixed point, Good, concrete in the creature, should overwhelm not without strife and wounds Evil concrete in the creature, and all things, "even the wicked," should be seen harmoniously blending in the glory of the attributes of God. The mythologic Pan, το πἁν the great Universal All, was deeply interested in the struggle: for the seed of the woman was to bruise the serpent's head; not merely as respected the small orb about to be, but concerning heaven itself, the unbounded "haysh hamaim," wherefrom dread Lucifer was thus to be ejected. On the earth, a mere planet of humble lustre, which the prouder suns around might well despise, was to be exhibited this noble and analogous result; the triumph of a lower intelligence, such as man, over a higher intelligence, such as angel: because, the former race, however frail, however weak, were to find their nature taken into God, and should have for their grand exemplar, leader and brother, the Very Lord of all arrayed in human guise; while the latter, the angelic fallen mass, in spite of all their pristine wisdom and excellency, were to set up as their captain him, who may well and philosophically be termed their Adversary.

This dark being, probably the mightiest of all mere creatures as the embodiment of corrupted good and perversion of an archangelic wisdom, was about to be suffered to fall victim to his own overtopping ambitions, and to drag with him a third part of the heavenly host—some tributary monarchs of the stars: thus he, and those his colleagues, should become a spectacle and a warning to all creatures else; to stand for spirits' reading in letters of fire a deeply burnt-in record how vast a gulf there is between the Maker and the made; how impassable a barrier between the derived intelligence and its infinite Creator. Such an unholy leader in rebellion against good—let us call him A or B, or why not for very euphony's sake Lucifer and Satanas?—such a corrupted excellence of heaven was to meet his final and inevitable disgrace to all eternity on the forthcoming battle-field of earth. Would it not be probable then that our world, soon to be fashioned and stocked with its teeming reasonable millions, should concentrate to itself the gaze of the universe, and, from the deeds to be done in it, should arrogate towards man a deep and fixed attention: that "the morning stars should sing together, and all the sons of God should shout for joy." Let us too, according to the power given to us, partake of such attention antecedently in some detail: albeit, as always, very little can be tracked of the length and breadth of our theme.

What would probably be the nature of such world and of such creatures, in a physical point of view? and what, in a moral point of view? It is not necessary to divide these questions: for the one so bears upon the other, or rather the latter so directs and pervades the former, that we may briefly treat of both as one.

The first probability would be, that, as the creature Man so to be abased and so to be exalted must be a responsible and reasonable being, every thing—with miraculous exceptions just enough to prove the rule—every thing around him should also be responsible and reasonable. In other words, that, with such exceptions as before alluded to, the whole texture of this world should bear to an inquisitive intellect the stamp of cause and effect: whilst for the mass, such cause and effect should be so little intrusive, that their easier religion might recognise God in all things immediately, rather than mediately. For instance: take the cases of stone, and of coal; the one so needful for man's architecture, the other for his culinary warmth. Now, however simple piety might well thank the Maker for having so stored earth with these for necessary uses; they ought, to a more learned, though not less pious ken, to seem not to have been created by an effort of the Great Father *quâ stone*, or *quâ coal*. Such a view might satisfy the ordinary mind: but thinkers would see no occasion for a miracle; when Christ raises Lazarus from the dead, it would have been a philosophical fault to have found the grave-clothes and swathing bandages ready loosened also. Unassisted man can do that: and unhelped common causes can generate stone and coal. The deposits of undated floods, the periodical currents of lava, the still and stagnant lake, and the furious up-bursting earthquake; all these would be called into play, and not the unrequired, I had almost said unreasonable, energies, which we call miracle. An agglutination of shells, once peopled with life; a crystallized lump of segregate minerals, once in a molten state; a mass of carbonated foliage and trunks of tropical trees, buried by long changes under the soil, wherever they had once waved greenly luxuriant; these, and no other, should have been man's stone and coal. This instance affects the reasonableness of such material creation. Take another, bearing upon its analogous responsibilities. As there was to be warred in this world the contest between good and evil, it would be expectable that the crust of man's earth, anteriorly to man's existence on it, should be marked with some traces that the evil, though newly born so far as might regard man's own disobedience, nevertheless had existed antecedently. In other words: it was probable that there should exist geological evidences of suffering and death: that the gigantic ichthyosaurus should be found fixed in rock with his cruel jaws closed upon his prey: that the fearful iguanodon should leave the tracks of having desolated a whole region of its reptile tribes: that volcanoes should have ravaged fair continents prolific of animal and vegetable life: that, in fine, though man's death came by man's sin, yet that death and sin were none of man's creating: he was only to draw down upon his head a prëexistent wo, an ante-toppling rock. Observe then, that these geological phenomena are only illustrations of my meaning: and whether such parables be true or false, the argument remains the same: we never build upon the sand of simile, but only use it here and there for strewing on the floor. Still, I will acknowledge that the introduction of such fossil instances appears to me wisely thrown in as affects their antecedent probability, because ignorant comments upon scriptural cosmogony have raised the absurdest objections against the truth of scriptural science. There is not a tittle of known geological fact, which is not absolutely reconcilable with Genesis and Job. But this is a word by the way: although aimed not without design against one of the poor and paltry weak-holds of the infidel.

ADAM.

REMEMBERING, then, that these are probabilities, and that the whole treatise purports to be nothing but a sketch, and not a finished picture, we have suggestively thus thrown out that the material world, man's home as man, was likely to have been prepared, as we posteriorly know it to be. Now, what of man's own person, circumstances, and individuality? Was it likely that the world should be stocked at once with many several races, or with one prolific seed? with a specimen of every variety of the genus man, or with the one generic type capable of forming those varieties?—Answer. One is by far the likelier in itself, because one thing must needs be more probable than many things: additionally; Wisdom and Power are always economical, and where one will suit the purpose, superfluities are rejected. That this one seed, covering with its product a various globe under all imaginable differences of circumstance and climate, should, in the lapse of ages, generate many species of the genus Man, was antecedently probable. For example, morality, peace and obedience would exercise transforming powers: their opposites the like in an opposite way. We can well fancy a mild and gentle race, as the Hindoo, to spring from the former educationals: and a family with flashing eyes and strongly-visaged natures, as the Malay, from a state of hatred, war, and license. We can well conceive that a tropical sun should carbonize some of that tender fabric the skin, adding also swift blood and fierce passions: while an arctic climate would induce a sluggish, stunted race. And, when to these considerations we add that of promiscuous unions, we arrive at the just likelihood that the whole family of man, though springing from one root, should, in the course of generations, be what now we see it.

Further. How should this prolific original, the first man, be created? and for a name let us call him Adam; a justly-chosen name enough, as alluding to his medium colour, ruddiness. Should he have been cast upon the ground an infant, utterly helpless, requiring miraculous aid and guidance at every turn? Should he be originated in boyhood, that hot and tumultuous time, when the creature is most rash, and least qualified for self-government? or should he be first discerned as an adult, in his prime, equal alike to obedience and rule, to moral control and moral energy?

Add also here; is it probable there would be any needless interval placed to procreations? or rather, should not such original seed be able immediately to fulfil the blank world call upon him, and as the greatly-teeming human father be found fitted from his birth to propagate his kind? The questions answer themselves.

Again. Should this first man have been discovered originally surrounded with all the appliances of an after-civilization, clad, and housed, and rendered artificial? nor rather, in a noble and naturally royal aspect appear on the stage of life as king of the natural creation, sole warder of a garden of fruits, with all his food thus readily concocted, and an eastern climate tempered to his nakedness?

Now, as to the solitariness of this one seed. From what we have already mused respecting God's benevolence, it would seem probable that the Maker might not see it good that man should be alone. The seed, originally one, proved (as was likely) to resemble its great parent, God, and to be partitionable, or reducible into persons; though with reasonable differences as between creature and Creator. Woman—Eve, the living or life-giving—was likely to have sprung out of the composite seed, Man, in order to companionship and fit society. Moreover, it were expectable that in the pattern creature, composite man, there should be involved some apt, mysterious typification of the same creature, after a fore-known fall restored, as in its perfect state of reünion with its Maker. *A posteriori*, the figurative notion is, that the Redeemed family, or mystical spouse, is incorporated in her husband, the Redeemer: not so much in the idea of marriage, as (taking election into view) of a cöcreation; as it were rib of rib, and life woven into life, not copulated or conjoined, but immingled in the being. This is a mystery most worthy of deep searching; a mystery deserving philosophic care, not less than the more unilluminate enjoyment of humble and believing Christians. I speak concerning Christ and his church.

THE FALL.

THERE is a special fitness in the fact, long since known and now to be perceived probable, that if mankind should fail in disobedience, it should rather be through the woman than through the man. Because, the man, *quâ man*, and the deputed head of all inferior creatures, was nearer to his Creator, than the woman; who, *quâ woman*, proceeded out of man. She was, so to speak, one step further from God, *ab origine*, than man was; therefore, more liable to err and fall away. To my own mind, I confess, it appears that nothing is more anteriorly probable than the plain, scriptural story of Adam and Eve: so simple that the child delights in it; so deep that the philosopher lingers there with an equal, but more reasonable joy.

For, let us now come to the probabilities of a temptation; and a fall; and what temptation; and how ordered.

The heavenly intelligences beheld the model-man and model-woman, rational beings, and in all points "very good." The Adversary panted for the fray, demanding some test of the obedience of this new, favourite race. And the Lord God was willing that the great controversy, which he foreknew, and for wise purposes allowed, should immediately commence. Where was the use of a delay? If you will reply, To give time to strengthen Adam's moral powers: I rejoin, he was made with more than enough of strength infused against any temptation not entering by the portal of his will: and against the open door of will neither time nor habits can avail. Moreover, the trial was to be exceedingly simple; no difficult abstinence, for man might freely eat of every thing but one; no natural passion tempted; no exertion of intelligence requisite. Adam lived in a garden; and his Maker, for proof of reasonable obedience, provides the most easy and obvious test of it—do not eat that apple. Was it, in reality, an improbable test; an unsuitable one? Was it not, rather, the likeliest in itself, and the fittest as addressed to the new-born, rational animal, which imagination could invent, or an amiable fore-knowledge of all things could desire? Had it been to climb some arduous height without looking back, or on no account to gaze upon the sun, how much less apt and easy of obedience! Thus much for the test.

Now, as to the temptation and its ordering. A creature, to be tempted fairly, must be tempted by another equal or lower creature; and through the senses. If mere spirit strives with spirit, plus matter, the strife is unequal: the latter is clogged; he has to fight in the net of Retiarius. But if both are netted, if both are spirit plus matter, (that is, material creatures,) there is no unfairness. Therefore, it would seem reasonable that the Adversary in person should descend from his mere spirituality into some tangible and humbled form. This could not well be man's, nor the semblance of man's: for the first pair would well know that they were all mankind: and, if the Lord God himself was accustomed to be seen of them as in a glorified humanity, it would be manifestly a moral incongruity to invest the devil in a similar form. It must, then, be the shape of some other creature; as a lion, or a lamb, or—why not a serpent? Is there any improbability here? and not rather as apt an avatar of the sinuous and wily rebel, the dangerous, fascinating foe, as poetry at least, nay, as any sterner contrivance could invent? The plain fact is, that Reason—given keenness—might have guessed this also antecedently a likelihood.

A few words more on other details probable to the temptation. Wonderful as it may seem to us with our present experience, in the case of the first woman it would scarcely excite her astonishment to be accosted in human phrase by one of the lower creatures; and in no other way could the tempter reach her mind. Much as Milton puts it, Eve sees a beautiful snake, eating, not improbably, of the forbidden apple. Attracted by a natural curiosity, she would draw near, and in a soft sweet voice the serpent, *i.e.* Lucifer in his guise, would whisper temptation. It was likely to have been keenly managed. Is it possible, O fair and favoured mistress of this beautiful garden, that your Maker has debarred you from its very choicest fruit? Only see its potencies for good: I, a poor reptile, am instantly thereby endued with knowledge and the privilege of speech. Am I dead for the eating?—ye shall not surely die; but shall become as gods yourselves; and this your Maker knoweth.

The marvellous fruit, invested thus with mystery, and tinctured with the secret charm of a thing unreasonably, nay, harmfully, forbidden, would then be allowed silently to plead its own merits. It was good for food: a young creature's first thought. It was pleasant to the eyes: addressing a higher sense than mere bodily appetite, than mental predilection for form and colour which marks fine breeding among men. It was also to be desired to make one wise; here was the climax, the great moral inducement which an innocent being might well be taken with; irrespectively of the one qualification that this wisdom was to be plucked in spite of God. Doubtless, it were probable, that had man not fallen, the knowledge of good would never have been long withheld: but he chose to reap the crop too soon, and reaped it mixed with tares, good, and evil.

I need not enlarge, in sermon form, upon the theme. It was probable that the weaker creature, Woman, once entrapped, she would have charms enough to snare her husband likewise: and the results thus perceived to have been likely, we have long since known for fact. That a depraved knowledge should immediately occasion some sort of clothing to be instituted by the great moral Governor, was likely: and there would be nothing near at hand, in fact nothing else suitable, but the skins of beasts. There is also a high probability that some sort of slaying should take place instantly on the fall, by way of reference to the coming sacrifice for sin; and for a type of some imputed righteousness. God covered Man's evil nakedness with the skins of innocent slain animals: even so, Blessed is he whose unrighteousness is forgiven, and whose sin is covered.

With respect to restoration from any such fall. There seems a remarkable prior probability for it, if we take into account the empty places in heaven, the vacant starry thrones which sin had caused to be untenanted. Just as, in after years, Israel entered into the cities and the gardens of the Canaanite and other seven nations, so it was anteriorly likely, would the ransomed race of Men come to be inheritors of the mansions among heavenly places, which had been left unoccupied by the fallen host of Lucifer. There was a gap to be filled: and probably there would be some better race to fill it.

THE FLOOD.

THEMES like those past and others still to come, are so immense, that each might fairly ask a volume for its separate elucidation. A few seeds, pregnant with thought, are all that we have here space, or time, or power to drop beside the world's highway. The grand outlines of our race command our first attention: we cannot stop to think and speak of every less detail. Therefore, now would I carry my companion across the patriarchal times at once to the era of the Deluge. Let us speculate, as hitherto, antecedently, throwing our minds as it were into some angelic prior state.

If, as we have seen probable, evil (a concretion always, not an abstraction) made some perceptible ravages even in the unbounded sphere of a heavenly creation, how much more rapid and overwhelming would its avalanche (once ill-commenced) be seen, when the site of its infliction was a poor band of men and women prisoned on a speck of earth. How likely was it that, in the lapse of no long time, the whole world should have been "corrupt before God, and filled with wickedness." How probable, that taking into account the great duration of pristine human life, the wicked family of man should speedily have festered up into an intolerable guiltiness. And was this dread result of the primal curse and disobedience to be regarded as the Adversary's triumph? Had this Accuser—the Saxon word is Devil—had this Slanderer of God's attribute then really beaten Good? or was not rather all this swarming sin an awful vindication to the universe of the great need-be that God unceasingly must hold his creature up lest he fall, and that out of Him is neither strength nor wisdom? Was Deity, either in Adam's case or this, baffled—nor rather justified? Was it an experiment which had really failed; nor rather one which, by its very seeming failure, proved the point in question, the misery of creatures when separate from God? Yea, the evil one was being beaten down beneath his very trophies in sad Tarpeian triumph: through conquest and his children's sins heightening his own misery.

Let us now advert to a few of the anterior probabilities affecting this evil earth's catastrophe. It is not competent to us to trench upon such ulterior views as are contained in the idea of types relatively to anti-types. Neither will we take the fanciful or poetical aspect of coming calamity, that earth, befouled with guilt, was likely to be washed clean by water. It is better to ask, as more relevant, in what other way more benevolent than drowning could, short of miracle, the race be made extinct? They were all to die in their sins, and swell in another sphere the miserable hosts of Satan. There was no hope for them, for there was no repentance. It was infinitely probable that God's long-suffering had worn out every reasonable effort for their restoration. They were then to die; but how?—in the least painful manner possible. Intestine wars, fevers, famines, a general burning-up of earth and all its millions, were any of these preferable sorts of death to that caused by the gradual rise of water, with hope of life accorded still even to the last gurgle? Assuredly, if "the tender mercies of the wicked are cruel," the judgments of the Good one are tempered well with mercy.

Moreover, in the midst of this universal slaughter there was one good seed to be preserved: and, as Heaven never works a miracle where common cause will suit the present purpose, it would have been inconsistent to have extirpated the wicked by any such means as must demonstrate the good to have been saved only by super-human agency.

The considerations of humanity, and of the divine less-intervention, add that of the natural and easy agency of a long-commissioned comet. No "*Deus e machinâ*" was needed for this effort: one of His ministers of flaming fire was charged to call forth the services of water. This was an easy and majestic interference. Ever since man fell—yea, ages before it—the omniscient eye of God had foreseen all things that should happen: and his ubiquity had, possibly from The Beginning, sped a comet on its errant way, which at a calculated period was to serve to wash the globe clean of its corruptions: was to strike the orbit of earth just in the moment of its passage, and disturbing by attraction the fountains of the great deep, was temporarily to raise their level. Was not this a just, a sublime, and a likely plan? Was it not a merciful, a perfect, and a worthy way? Who should else have buried the carcases on those fierce battle-fields, or the mouldering heaps of pestilence and famine?—But, when at Jehovah's summons, heaving to the comet's mass, the pure and mighty sea rises indignant from its bed, by drowning to cleanse the foul and mighty land—how easy an engulfing of the corpses; how awful that universal burial; how apt their monumental epitaph written in water, "The wicked are like the troubled sea that cannot rest;" how dread the everlasting requiem chanted for the whelmed race by the waves roaring above them: yea, roaring above them still! for in that chaotic hour it seems probable to reason that the land changed place with ocean; thus giving the new family of man a fresh young world to live upon.

NOAH.

WHEN the world, about to grow so wicked, was likely thus to have been cleansed, and so renewed, the great experiment of man's possible righteousness was probable to be repeated in another form. We may fancy some high angelic mind to have gone through some such line of thought as this, respecting the battle and combatants. Were those champions, Lucifer and Adam, really fit to be matched together? Was the tourney just; were the weapons equal; was it, after all, a fair fight?—on one side, the fallen spirit, mighty still, though fallen, subtlest, most unscrupulous, most malicious, exerting every energy to rear a rebel kingdom against God; on the other, a new-born, inexperienced, innocent, and trustful creature, a poor man vexed with appetites, and as naked for absolute knowledge in his mind as for garments on his body. Was it, in this view of the case, an equal contest? were the weapons of that warfare matched and measured fairly?

Some such objection, we may suppose, might seem to have been admissible, as having a show at least of reason: and, after the world was to have been cleansed of all its creatures in the manner I have mentioned, a new champion is armed for the conflict, totally different in every respect; and to reason's view vastly superior.

This time, the Adam of renewed earth is to be the best and wisest, nay, the only good and wise one of the whole lost family: a man, with the experience of full six hundred years upon his hoary brow, with the unspeakable advantage of having walked with God all those long-drawn centuries, a patriarch of twenty generations, recognised as the one great and faithful witness, the only worshipper and friend of his Creator. Could a finer sample be conceived? was not Noah the only spark of spiritual "consolation" in the midst of earth's dark death? and was not he the best imaginable champion to stand against the wiles of the devil? Verily, reason might have guessed, that if Deity saw fit to renew the fight at all, the representative of man should have been Noah.

Before we touch upon the immediate fall of this new Adam also, at a time when God and reason had deserted him, it will be more orderly to allude to the circumstances of his preservation in the flood. How, in such a hurlyburly of the elements, should the chosen seed survive? No house, nor hill-top, no ordinary ship would serve the purpose: still less the unreasonable plan of any cavern hermetically sealed, or any aerial chariot miraculously lifted up above the lower firmament. To use plain and simple words, I can fancy no wiser method than a something between a house and a diving-bell; a vessel, entirely storm-tight and water-tight, which nevertheless for necessary air should have an open window at the top: say, one a cubit square. This, properly hooded against deluging rain, and supplied with such helps to ventilation as leathern pipes, air tunnels and similar appliances, would not be an impracticable method. However, instead of being under water as a diving-bell, the vessel would be better made to float upon the rising flood, and thus continually keeping its level, would be ready to strike land as the waters assuaged.

Now, as to the size of this ark, this floating caravan, it must needs be very large; and also take a great time in building. For, suffering cause and effect to go on without a new creation, it was reasonable to suppose that the man, so launching as for another world on the ocean of existence, would take with him (especially if God's benevolence so ordered it) all the known appliances of civilized life; as well as a pair or two of every creature he could collect, to stock withal the renewed earth according to their various excellences in their kinds. The lengthy, arduous, and expensive preparation of this mighty ark—a vessel which must include forests of timber and consume generations in building; besides the world-be-known collection of all manner of strange animals for the stranger fancy of a fanatical old man; not to mention also the hoary Preacher's own century of exhortations: with how great moral force all this living warning would be calculated to act upon the world of wickedness and doom! Here was the great ante-diluvian potentate, Noah, a patriarch of ages, wealthy beyond our calculations—(for how else without a needless succession of miracles could he have built and stocked the ark?)—a man of enormous substance, good report, and exalted station, here was he for a hundred and twenty years engaged among crowds of unbelieving workmen, in constructing a most extravagant ship, which, forsooth, filled with samples of all this world's stores, was to sail with our only good family in search of a better. Moreover, Noah here declares that our dear old mother-earth is to be destroyed for her iniquities by rain and sea: and he exhorts us by a solid evidence of his own faith at least, if by nothing else, to repent, and turn to him, whom Abel, Seth, and Enoch, as well as this good Noah, represent as our Maker. Would not such sneers and taunts be probable: would they not amply vindicate the coming judgment? Was not the "long-suffering of God" likely to have thus been tried "while the ark was preparing?" and when the catastrophe should come, had not that evil generation been duly warned against it? On the whole, it would have been Reason's guess that Noah should be saved as he was; that the ark should have been as we read of it in Genesis; and that the very immensity of its construction should have served for a preaching to mankind. As to any idea that the ark is an unreasonable (some have even said ridiculous) incident to the deluge, it seems to me to have furnished a clear case of antecedent probability.

Lastly: Noah's fall was very likely to have happened: not merely in the theological view of the matter, as an illustration of the truth that no human being can stand fast in righteousness: but from the just consideration that he imported with him the seeds of an impure state of society, the remembered luxuries of that old world. For instance, among the plants of earth which Noah would have preserved for future insertion in the soil, he could not have well forgotten the generous, treacherous Vine. That to a righteous man, little used to all unhallowed sources of exhilaration, this should have been a stepping-stone to a defalcation from God, was likely. It was probable in itself, and shows the honesty as well as the verisimilitude of Scripture to read, that "Noah began to be a husbandman, and planted a vineyard; and he drank of the wine, and was drunken." There was nothing here but what, taking all things into consideration, Reason might have previously guessed. Why then withhold the easier matter of an afterward belief?

BABEL.

THIS book ought to be read, as mentally it is written, with at the end of every sentence one of those *et ceteras*, which the genius of a Coke interpreted so keenly of the genius of a Littleton: for, far more remains on each subject to be said, than in any one has been attempted.

Let us pass on to the story of Babel: I can conceive nothing more *à priori* probable than the account we read in Scripture. Briefly consider the matter. A multitude of men, possibly the then whole human family, once more a fallen race, emigrate towards the East, and come to a vast plain in the region of Shinar, afterwards Chaldæa. Fertile, well-watered, apt for every mundane purpose, it yet wanted one great requisite. The degenerate race "put not their trust in God:" they did not believe but that the world might some day be again destroyed by water: and they required a point of refuge in the possible event of a second deluge from the broken bounds of ocean and the windows of the skies. They had come from the West; more strictly the North-west, a land of mountains, as they deemed them, ready-made refuges: and their scheme, a probable one enough, was to construct some such mountain artificially, so that its top might reach the clouds, as did the summit of Ararat. This would serve the twofold purpose of outwitting any further attempt to drown them, and of making for themselves a proud name upon the earth. So, the Lord God, in his etherealized human form (having taken counsel with His own divine compeers), coming in the guise wherein He was wont to walk with Adam and with Enoch and his other saints of men, "came down and saw the tower:" truly, He needed not have come, for ubiquity was his, and omniscience; but in the days when God and man were (so to speak) less chronologically divided than as now, and while yet the trial-family was young, it does not seem unlikely that He should. God then, in his aspect of the Head of all mankind, took notice of that dangerous and unholy combination: and He made within His Triune Mind the wise resolve to break their bond of union. Omniscience had herein a view to ulterior consequences benevolent to man, and He knew that it would be a wise thing for the future world, as well as a discriminative check upon the race then living, to confuse the universal language into many discordant dialects. Was this in any sense an improbable or improper method of making "the devices of the wicked to be of none effect, and of laughing to scorn the counsels of the mighty?" Was it not to have been expected that a fallen race should be disallowed the combinative force necessary to a common language, but that such force should be dissipated and diverted for moral usages into many tongues?—There they were, all the chiefs of men congregated to accomplish a vast, ungodly scheme: and interposing Heaven to crush such insane presumption—and withal thereafter designing to bless by arranging through such means the future interchange of commerce and the enterprise of nationalities—He, in his Trinity, was not unlikely to have said, "Let us go down, and confound their language." What better mode could have been devised to scatter mankind, and so to people the extremities of earth? In order that the various dialects should crystallize apart, each in its discriminative lump, the nucleus of a nation; that thereafter the world might be able no longer to unite as one man against its Lord, but by conflicting interests, the product of conflicting languages, might give to good a better chance of not being altogether overwhelmed; that, though many "a multitude might go to do evil," it should not thenceforward be the whole consenting family of man; but that, here by one and there by one, the remembrance of God should be kept extant, and evil no longer acquire an accumulated force, by having all the world one nation.

JOB.

EVERY scriptural incident and every scriptural worthy deserves its own particular discussion: and might easily obtain it. For example; the anterior probability that human life in patriarchal times should have been very much prolonged, was obvious; from consideration of—1, the benevolence of God; 2, the inexperience of man; and 3, the claim so young a world would hold upon each of its inhabitants: whilst Holy Writ itself has prepared an answer to the probable objection, that the years were lunar years, or months; by recording that Arphaxad and Salah and Eber and Peleg and Reu and Serug and Nahor, descendants of Shem, each had children at the average age of two-and-thirty, and yet the lives of all varied in duration from a hundred and fifty years to five hundred. And many similar credibilities might be alluded to: what shall I say of Abraham's sacrifice, of Moses and the burning bush, of Jonah also, and Elisha, and of the prophets? for the time would fail me to tell how probable and simple in each instance is its deep and marvellous history. There is food for philosophic thought in every page of ancient Jewish Scripture scarcely less than in those of primitive Christianity: here, after our fashion, we have only touched upon a sample.

The opening scene to the book of Job has vexed the faith of many very needlessly: to my mind, nothing was more likely to have literally and really happened. It is one of those few places where we get an insight into what is going on elsewhere: it is a lifting off the curtain of eternity for once, revealing the magnificent simplicities constantly presented in the halls of heaven. And I am moved to speak about it here, because I think a plain statement of its sublime probabilities will be acceptable to many: especially if they have been harassed by the doubts of learned men respecting the authorship of that rare history. It signifies nothing who recorded the circumstances and conversations, so long as they were true, and really happened: given power, opportunity, and honesty, a life of Dr. Johnson would be just as fair in fact, if written by Smollett, as by Boswell, or himself. Whether then Job, the wealthy prince of Uz, or Abraham, or Moses, or Elisha, or Eliphaz, or whoever else, have placed the words on record, there they stand, true; and the whole book in all its points was anteriorly likely to have been decreed a component part of revelation. Without it, there would have been wanting some evidence of a godly worship among men through the long and dreary interval of several hundred years: there would never have been given for man's help the example of a fortitude, and patience, and trust in God most brilliant; of a faith in the resurrection and redeemer, signal and definite beyond all other texts in Jewish Scripture: as well as of a human knowledge of God in his works beyond all modern instance. However, the excellences of that narrative are scarcely our theme: we return to the starting-post of its probability, especially with reference to its supernatural commencement. What we have shown credible, many pages back, respecting good and evil and the denizens of heaven, finds a remarkable after-proof in the two first chapters of Job; and for some such reason, by reference, these two chapters were themselves anteriorly to have been expected.

Let us see what happened:

"There was a day when the sons of God came to present themselves before the Lord, and Satan came also among them. And the Lord said unto Satan, whence comest thou? Then Satan answered the Lord, and said, From going to and fro in the earth, and from walking up and down in it. And the Lord said unto Satan, Hast thou considered my servant Job, that there is none like him in the earth, a perfect and an upright man, one that feareth God and escheweth evil? Then Satan answered the Lord, and said, Doth Job fear God for naught? Hast thou not made a hedge about him, and about his house, and about all that he hath on every side? Thou hast blessed the work of his hands, and his substance is increased in the land. But put forth thine hand now, and touch all he hath, and he will curse thee to thy face. And the Lord said unto Satan, Behold, all that he hath is in thy power; only upon himself put not forth thine hand. So Satan went forth from the presence of the Lord."—[Job 1. 6-13.]

It is a most stately drama: any paraphrase would spoil its dignity, its quiet truth, its unpretending, yet gigantic lineaments. Note: in allusion to our views of evil, that Satan also comes among the sons of God: note, the generous dependence placed by a generous Master on his servant well-upheld by that Master's own free grace: note, Satan's constant imputation against piety when blessed of God with worldly wealth, Doth he serve for naught? I can discern no cause wherefore all this scene should not have truly happened; not as in vision of some holy man, but as in fact. Let us read on, before further comment:

"Again, there was a day when the sons of God came to present themselves before the Lord, and Satan came also among them to present himself before the Lord. And the Lord said unto Satan, Whence comest thou? And Satan answered the Lord, and said, From going to and fro in the earth, and from walking up and down in it. And the Lord said unto Satan, Hast thou considered my servant Job, that there is none like him in the earth, a perfect and an upright man, one that feareth God and escheweth evil? and still he holdeth fast his integrity, although thou movedst me against him, to destroy him without cause. And Satan answered the Lord, and said, Skin for skin, yea, all that a man hath will he give for his life. But put forth thine hand now, and touch his bone and his flesh, and he will curse thee to thy face. And the Lord said unto Satan, Behold, he is in thine hand; but save his life. So Satan went forth from the presence of the Lord, and smote Job with sore boils, from the sole of his foot unto his crown."

Some such scene, displaying the devil's malice, slandering sneers, and permitted power, recommends itself to my mind as antecedently to have been looked for: in order that we might know from what quarter many of life's evils come; with what aims and ends they are directed; what limits are opposed to our foe; and Who is on our side. We needed some such insight into the heavenly places; some such hint of what is continually going on before the Lord's tribunal; we wanted this plain and simple setting forth of good and evil in personal encounter, of innocence awhile given up to malice for its chastening and its triumph. Lo, all this so probable scene is here laid open to us, and many, against reason, disbelieve it!

Note, in allusion to our after-theme, the *locus* of heaven, that there is some such usual place of periodical gathering. Note, the open unchiding loveliness dwelling in the Good One's words, as contrasted with the subtle, slanderous hatred of the Evil. And then the vulgar proverb, Skin for skin: this pious Job is so intensely selfish, that let him lose what he may, he heeds it not; he cares for nothing out of his own skin. And there are many more such notabilities.

Why did I produce these passages at length? For their Doric simplicity; for their plain and masculine features; for their obvious truthfulness; for their manifest probability as to fact, and expectability previously to it. Why on earth should they be doubted in their literal sense? and were they not more likely to have happened than to have been invented? We have no such geniuses now as this writer must have been, who by the pure force of imagination could have created that tableau. Milton had Job to go to. Simplicity is proof presumptive in favour of the plain inspiration of such passages: for the plastic mind which could conceive so just a sketch, would never have rested satisfied, without having painted and adorned it picturesquely. Such rare flights of fancy are always made the most of.

One or two thoughts respecting Job's trial. That he should at last give way, was only probable: he was, in short, another Adam, and had another fall; albeit he wrestled nobly. Worthy was he to be named among God's chosen three, "Noah, Daniel, and Job:" and worthy that the Lord should bless his latter end. This word brings me to the point I wish to touch on; the great compensation which God gave to Job.

Children can never be regarded as other than individualities: and notwithstanding Eastern feelings about increase in quantity, its quality is, after all, the question for the heart. I mean that many children to be born, is but an inadequate return for many children dying. If a father loses a well-beloved son, it is small recompense of that aching void that he gets another. For this reason of the affections, and because I suppose that thinkers have sympathized with me in the difficulty, I wish to say a word about Job's children, lost and found. It will clear away what is to some minds a moral and affectionate objection. Now, this is the state of the case.

The patriarch is introduced to us as possessing so many camels, and oxen, and so forth; and ten children. All these are represented to him by witnesses, to all appearance credible, as dead; and he mourns for his great loss accordingly. Would not a merchant feel to all intents and purposes a ruined man, if he received a clear intelligence from different parts of the world at once that all his ships and warehouses had been destroyed by hurricanes and fire? Faith given, patience follows: and the trial is morally the same, whether the news be true or false. Remarkably enough, after the calamitous time is past, when the good man of Uz is discerned as rewarded by heaven for his patience by the double of every thing once lost—his children remain the same in number, ten. It seems to me quite possible that neither camels, &c., nor children, really had been killed. Satan might have meant it so, and schemed it; and the singly-coming messengers believed it all, as also did the well-enduring Job. But the scriptural word does not go to say that these things happened; but that certain emissaries said they happened. I think the devil missed his mark: that the messengers were scared by some abortive diabolic efforts; and that, (with a natural increase of camels, &c., meanwhile,) the patriarch's paternal heart was more than compensated at the last, by the restoration of his own dear children. They were dead, and are alive again; they were lost, and are found. Like Abraham returning from Mount Calvary with Isaac, it was the Resurrection in a figure.

If to this view objection is made, that, because the boils of Job were real, therefore, similarly real must be all his other evils; I reply, that in the one temptation, the suffering was to be mental; in the other, bodily. In the latter case, positive, personal pain, was the gist of the matter: in the former, the heart might be pierced, and the mind be overwhelmed, without the necessity of any such incurable affliction as children's deaths amount to. God's mercy may well have allowed the evil one to overreach himself; and when the restoration came, how double was the joy of Job over those ten dear children.

Again, if any one will urge that, in the common view of the case, Job at the last really has twice as many children as before, for that he has ten old ones in heaven, and ten new ones on earth: I must, in answer, think that explanation as unsatisfactory to us, as the verity of it would have been to Job. Affection, human affection, is not so numerically nor vicariously consoled: and it is, perhaps, worth while here to have thrown out (what I suppose to be) a new view of the case, if only to rescue such wealth as children from the infidel's sneer of being confounded with such wealth as camels. Moreover, such a paternal reward was anteriorly more probable.

JOSHUA.

HOW many of our superficial thinkers have been staggered at the great miracle recorded of Joshua; and how few, even of the deeper sort, comparatively, may have discerned its aptness, its science, and its anterior likelihood: "Sun! stand thou still upon Gibeon; and thou, moon, in the valley of Ajalon." Now, consider, for we hope to vindicate even this stupendous event from the charge of improbability.

Baal and Ashtaroth, chief idols of the Canaanites, were names for sun and moon. It would manifestly be the object of God and His ambassador to cast utter scorn on such idolatry. And what could be more apt than that Joshua, commissioned to extirpate the corrupted race, should miraculously be enabled, as it were, to bind their own gods to aid in the destruction of such votaries?

Again: what should Joshua want with the moon for daylight, to help him to rout the foes of God more fiercely? Why not, according to the astronomical ignorance of those days, let her sail away, unconsorted by the sun, far beyond the valley of Ajalon? There was a reason, here, of secret, unobtruded science: if the sun stopped, the moon must stop too; that is to say, both apparently: the fact being that the earth must, for the while, rest on its axis. This, I say, is a latent, scientific hint; and so, likewise, is the accompanying mention as a fact, that the Lord immediately "rained great stones out of heaven" upon the flying host. For would it not be the case that, if the diurnal rotation of earth were suddenly to stop, the impetus of motion would avail to raise high into the air by centrifugal force, and fling down again by gravity, such unanchored things as fragments of rock?

Once more: our objector will here perhaps inquire, Why not then command the earth to stop—and not the sun and moon? if thus probably Joshua or his Inspirer knew better? Answer. Only let a reasonable man consider what would have been the moral lesson both to Israelite and to Canaanite, if the great successor of Moses had called out, incomprehensibly to all, "Earth, stand thou still on thine axis;"—and lo! as if in utter defiance of such presumption, and to vindicate openly the heathen gods against the Jewish, the very sun and moon in heaven stopped, and glared on the offender. I question whether such a noon-day miracle might not have perverted to idolatry the whole believing host: and almost reasonably too. The strictly philosophical terms would have entirely nullified the whole moral influence. God in his word never suffers science to hinder the progress of truth: a worldly philosophy does this almost in every instance, darkening knowledge with a cloud of words: but the science of the Bible is usually concealed in some neighbouring hint quite handy to the record of the phenomena expressed in ordinary language. In fact, for all common purposes, no astronomer finds fault with such phrases as the moon rising, or the sun setting: he speaks according to the appearance, though he knows perfectly well that the earth is the cause of it, and not the sun or moon. Carry this out in Joshua's case.

On the whole, the miracle was very plain, very comprehensible, and very probable. It had good cause: for Canaan felt more confidence in the protection of his great and glorious Baal, than stiff-necked Judah in his barely-seen divinity: and surely it was wise to vindicate the true but invisible God by the humiliation of the false and far-seen idol. This would constitute to all nations the quickly-rumoured proof that Jehovah of the Israelites was God in heaven above as well as on the earth beneath. And, considering the peculiar idolatries of Canaan, it seems to me that no miracle could have been better placed and better timed—in other words, anteriorly more probable—than the command of obedience to the sun and to the moon. I suppose that few persons who read this book will be unaware, that the circumstance is alluded to as well in that honest heathen, old Herodotus, as in the learned Jew Josephus. The volumes are not near me for reference to quotations: but such is fact: it will be found in Herodotus, about the middle of Euterpe, connected with an allusion to the analogous case of Hezekiah.

No miracles, on the whole (to take one after-view of the matter), could have been better tested: for two armies (not to mention all surrounding countries) must have seen it plainly and clearly: if then it had never occurred, what a very needless exposure of the falsity of the Jewish Scriptures! These were open, published writings, accessible to all: Cyrus and Darius and Alexander read them, and Ethiopian eunuchs; Parthians, Medes, and Elamites, with all other nations of the earth, had free access to those records. Only imagine if some recent history of England, Adolphus's, or Stebbing's, contained an account of a certain day in George the Fourth's reign having had twenty-four hour's daylight instead of the usual admixture; could the intolerable falsehood last a minute? Such a placard would be torn away from the records of the land the moment a rash hand had fixed it there. But, if the matter were fact, how could any historian neglect it?—In one sense, the very improbability of such a marvel being recorded, argues the probability of it having actually occurred.

Much more might here be added: but our errand is accomplished, if any stumbling-block had been thus easily removed from some erring thinker's path. Surely, we have given him some reason for faith's due acceptance of Joshua's miracle.

THE INCARNATION.

IN touching some of the probabilities of our blessed Lord's career, it would be difficult to introduce and illustrate the subject better, than by the following anecdote. Whence it is derived, has escaped my memory; but I have a floating notion that it is told of Socrates in Xenophon or Plato. At any rate, by way of giving fixity thereto and picturesqueness, let us here report the story as of the Athenian Solomon:

Surrounded by his pupils, the great heathen Reasoner was being questioned and answering questions: in particular respecting the probability that the universal God would be revealed to his creatures. "What a glorious King would he appear!" said one, possibly the brilliant Alcibiades: "What a form of surpassing beauty!" said another, not unlikely the softer Crito. "Not so, my children," answered Socrates. "Kings and the beautiful are few, and the God, if he came on earth as an exemplar, would in shape and station be like the greater number." "Indeed, Master? then how should he fail of being made a King of men, for his goodness, and his majesty, and wisdom?" "Alas! my children," was pure Reason's just rejoinder, "[Greek: oi pleiones kakoi], most men are so wicked that they would hate his purity, despise his wisdom, and as for his majesty, they could not truly see it. They might indeed admire for a time, but thereafter (if the God allowed it), they would even hunt and persecute and kill him." "Kill him!" exclaimed the eager group of listeners; "kill Him? how should they, how could they, how dare they kill God?" "I did not say, kill God," would have been wise Socrates's reply, "for God existeth ever: but men in enmity and envy might even be allowed to kill that human form wherein God walked for an ensample. That they could, were God's humility: that they should, were their own malice: that they dared, were their own grievous sin and peril of destruction. Yea," went on the keen-eyed sage, "men would slay him by some disgraceful death, some lingering, open, and cruel death, even such as the death of slaves!"—Now slaves, when convicted of capital crime, were always crucified.

Whatever be thought of the genuineness of the anecdote, its uses are the same to us. Reason might have arrived at the salient points of Christ's career, and at His crucifixion!

I will add another topic: How should the God on earth arrive there? We have shown that His form would probably be such as man's; but was he to descend bodily from the atmosphere at the age of full-grown perfection, or to rise up out of the ground with earthquakes and fire, or to appear on a sudden in the midst of the market-place, or to come with legions of his heavenly host to visit his Temple? There was a wiser way than these, more reasonable, probable, and useful. Man required an exemplar for every stage of his existence up to the perfection of his frame. The infant, and the child, and the youth, would all desire the human-God to understand their eras; they would all, if generous and such as he would love, long to feel that He has sympathy with them in every early trial, as in every later grief. Moreover, the God coming down with supernatural glories or terrors would be a needless expense of ostentatious power. He, whose advent is intended for the encouragement of men to exercise their reason and their conscience; whose exhortation is "he that hath ears to hear, let him hear;" that pure Being, who is the chief preacher of Humility, and the great teacher of man's responsible condition—surely, he would hardly come in any way astoundingly miraculous, addressing his advent not to faith, but to sight, and challenging the impossibility of unbelief by a galaxy of spiritual wonders. Yet, if He is to come at all—and a word or two of this hereafter—it must be either in some such strange way; or in the usual human way; or in a just admixture of both. As the first is needlessly overwhelming to the responsible state of man, so the second is needlessly derogatory to the pure essence of God; and the third idea would seem to be most probable. Let us guess it out. Why should not this highest Object of faith and this lowest Subject of obedience be born, seemingly by human means, but really by divine? Why should there not be found some unspotted holy virgin, betrothed to a just man and soon to be his wife, who, by the creative power of Divinity, should miraculously conceive the shape divine, which God himself resolved to dwell in? Why should she not come of a lineage and family which for centuries before had held such expectation? Why should not the just man, her affianced, who had never known her yet, being warned of God in a dream of this strange, immaculate conception, "fear not to take unto him Mary his wife," lest the unbelieving world should breathe slander on her purity, albeit he should really know her not until after the Holy Birth. There is nothing unreasonable here; every step is previously credible: and invention's self would be puzzled to devise a better scheme. The Virgin-born would thus be a link between God and man, the great Mediator: his natures would fulfil every condition required of their double and their intimate conjunction. He would have arrived at humanity without its gross beginnings, and have veiled his Godhead for a while in a pure though mortal tenement. He would have participated in all the tenderness of woman's nature, and thus have reached the keenest sensibilities of men.

Themes such as these are inexhaustible: and I am perpetually conscious of so much left unsaid, that at every section I seem to have said next to nothing. Nevertheless, let it go; the good seed yet shall germinate. "Cast thy bread upon the waters, and thou shall find it after many days."

It may to some minds be a desideratum, to allude to the anterior probability that God should come in the flesh. Much of this has been anticipated under the head of Visible Deity and elsewhere; as this treatise is so short, one may reasonably expect every reader to take it in regular course. For additional considerations: the Benevolent Maker would hardly leave his creatures to perish, without one word of warning or one gleam of knowledge. The question of the Bible is considered further on: but exclusively of written rules and dogmas, it was likely that Our Father should commission chosen servants of his own, orally to teach and admonish; because it would be in accordance with man's reasonable nature, that he should best and easiest learn from the teaching his brethren. So then, after all lesser ambassadors had failed, it was to be expected that He should send the highest one of all, saying, "They will reverence my Son." We know that this really did occur by innumerable proofs, and wonderful signs posterior: and now, after the event, we discern it to have been anteriorly probable.

It was also probable in another light. This world is a world of incarnations; nothing has a real and potential existence, which is not embodied in some form. A theory is nothing; if no personal philosopher, no sect, or school of learners, takes it up. An opinion is mere air; without the multitude to give it all the force of a mighty wind. An idea is mere spiritual light; if unclad in deeds, or in words written or spoken. So, also, of the Godhead: He would be like all these. He would pervade words spoken, as by prophets or preachers: He would include words written, as in the Bible: He would influence crowds with spirit-stirring sentiments: He would embody the theory of all things in one simple, philosophic form. As this material world is constituted, God could not reveal himself at all, excepting by the aid of matter. I mean; even granting that He spiritually inspired a prophet, still the man was necessary: he becomes an inspired man; not mere inspiration. So, also, of a book; which is the written labour of inspired men. There is no doing without the Humanity of God, so far as this world is concerned, any more than His Deity can be dispensed with, regarding the worlds beyond worlds, and the ages of ages, and the dread for ever and ever.

MAHOMETANISM.

IT seems expedient that, in one or two instances, I should attempt the illustration of this rule of probability in matters beyond the Bible. As very fair ones, take Mahometanism and Romanism. And first of the former.

At the commencement of the seventh century, or a little previously to that era, we know that a fierce religion sprang up, promulgated by a false prophet. I wish briefly to show that this was antecedently to have been expected.

In a moral point of view, the Christian world, torn by all manner of schisms, and polluted by all sorts of heresies, had earned for the human race, whether accepting the gospel or refusing it, some signal and extensive punishment at the hands of Him, who is the Great Retributor as well as the Munificent Rewarder. In a physical point of view, the civilized kingdoms of the earth had become stagnant, arguing that corrupt and poisonous calm which is the herald of a coming tempest. The heat of a true religion had cooled down into lukewarm disputations about nothings, scholastical and casuistic figments; whilst at the same time the prevalence of peaceful doctrines had amalgamated all classes into a luxurious indolence. Passionate Man is not to be so satisfied; and the time was fully come for the rise of some fierce spirit, who should change the tinsel theology of the crucifix for the iron religion of the sword: who should blow in the ears of the slumbering West the shrill war-blast of Eastern fervencies; who should exchange the dull rewards of canonization due to penance, or an after-life voluntary humiliation under pseudo-saints and angels, for the human and comprehensible joys of animal appetite and military glory: who should enlist under his banner all the frantic zeal, all the pent-up licentiousness, all the heart-burning hatreds of mankind, stifled either by a positive barbarism, or the incense-laden cloud of a scarcely-masked idolatry.

Thus, and then, was likely to arise a bold and self-confiding hero, leaning on his own sword: a man of dark sentences, who, by judiciously pilfering from this quarter and from that shreds of truth to jewel his black vestments of error, and by openly proclaiming that Oneness of the object of all worship which besotted Christendom had then, from undue reverence to saints and martyrs, virgins and archangels, well nigh forgotten; a man who, by pandering to human passions and setting wide as virtue's avenue the flower-tricked gates of vice; should thus, like Lucifer before him, in a comet-like career of victory, sweep the startled firmament of earth, and drag to his erratic orbit the stars of heaven from their courses.

Mahomet; his humble beginnings; his iron perseverance under early probable checks; his blind, yet not all unsublime, dependence on fatality; his ruthless, yet not all undeserved, infliction of fire and sword upon the cowering coward race that filled the western world;—these, and all whatever else besides attended his train of triumphs, and all whatever besides has lasted among Moors, and Arabs, and Turks, and Asiatics, even to this our day—constitute to a thinking mind (and it seems not without cause) another antecedent probability. Let the scoffer about Mahomet's success, and the admirer of his hotchpot Koran; let him to whom it is a stumbling-block that error (if indeed, quoth he, it be more erroneous than what Christendom counts truth) should have had such free course and been glorified, while so-called Truth, *pede claudo*, has limped on even as now cautiously and ingloriously through the well-suspicious world; let him who thinks he sees in Mahomet's success an answer to the foolish argument of some, who test the truth of Christianity by its Gentile triumphs; let him ponder these things. Reason, the God of his idolatry, might, with an archangel's ken, have prophesied some Mahomet's career: and, so far from such being in the nature of any objection to Faith, the idea thus thrown out, well-mused upon, will be seen to lend Faith an aid in the way of previous likelihood.

"There is one God, and Mahomet is his prophet!" How admirably calculated such a war-cry would be for the circumstances of the seventh century. The simple sublimity of Oneness, as opposed to school-theology and catholic demons: the glitter of barbaric pomp, instead of tame observances: the flashing scimetar of ambition to supersede the cross: a turban aigretted with jewels for the twisted wreath of thorns. As human nature is, and especially in that time was, nothing was more expectable (even if prophetic records had not taught it), than the rise and progress of that great False Prophet, whose waving crescent even now blights the third part of earth.

ROMANISM.

WE all know how easy it is to prophesy after the event: but it would be uncandid and untrue to confound this remark with another, cousin-germane to it; to wit: how easy it is to discern of any event, after it has happened, whether or not it were antecedently likely. When the race is over, and the best horse has won (or by clever jockey-management, the worst), how obviously could any gentleman on the turf, now in possession of particulars, have seen the event to have been so probable, that he would have staked all upon its issue.

Carry out this familiar idea; which, as human nature goes, is none the weaker as to illustration, because it is built upon the rule "*parvis componere magna*." Let us sketch a line or two of that great fore-shadowing cartoon, the probabilities of Romanism.

That our blessed Master, even in His state as man, beheld its evil characteristics looming on the future, seems likely not alone from both His human keenness and His divine omniscience, but from here and there a hint dropped in his biography. Why should He, on several occasions, have seemed, I will say with some apparent sharpness, to have rebuked His virgin mother.—"Woman, what have I to do with thee?"—"Who are my mother and my brethren?"—"Yea—More blessed than the womb which bare me, and the paps that I have sucked, is the humblest of my true disciples." Let no one misunderstand me: full well I know the just explanations which palliate such passages; and the love stronger than death which beat in that Filial heart. But, take the phrases as they stand; and do they not in reason constitute some warning and some prophecy that men should idolize the mother? Nothing, in fact, was more likely than that a just human reverence to the most favoured among women should have increased into her admiring worship: until the humble and holy Mary, with the sword of human anguish at her heart, should become exaggerated and idealized into Mother of God—instead of Jesus's human matrix, Queen of heaven, instead of a ransomed soul herself, the joy of angels—in lieu of their lowly fellow-worshipper, and the Rapture of the blessed—thus dethroning the Almighty.

Take a second instance: why should Peter, the most loving, most generous, most devoted of them all, have been singled out from among the twelve—with a "Get thee behind me, Satan?"—it really had a harsh appearance; if it were not that, prophetically speaking, and not personally, he was set in the same category with Judas, the "one who was a devil." I know the glosses, and the contexts, and the whole amount of it. Folios have been written, and may be written again, to disprove the text; but the more words, the less sense: it stands, a record graven in the Rock; that same Petra, whereon, as firm and faithful found, our Lord Jesus built his early Church: it stands, a mark indelibly burnt into that hand, to whom were intrusted, not more specially than to any other of the saintly sent, the keys of the kingdom of heaven: it stands, along with the same Peter's deep and terrible apostacy, a living witness against some future Church, who should set up this same Peter as the Jupiter of their Pantheon: who should positively be idolizing now an image christened Peter, which did duty two thousand years ago as a statue of Libyan Jove! But even this glaring compromise was a matter probable, with the data of human ambitions, and a rotten Christianity.

Examples such as these might well be multiplied: bear with a word or two more, remembering always that the half is not said which might be said in proof; nor in answering the heap of frivolous objections.

Why, unless relics and pseudo-sacred clothes were to be prophetically humbled into their own mere dust and nothing-worthiness, why should the rude Roman soldiery have been suffered to cast lots for that vestment, which, if ever spiritual holiness could have been infused into mere matter, must indeed have remained a relic worthy of undoubted worship? It was warm with the Animal heat of the Man inhabited by God: it was half worn out in the service of His humble travels, and had even, on many occasions, been the road by which virtue had gone out; not of it, but of Him. What! was this wonderful robe to work no miracles? was it not to be regarded as a sort of outpost of the being who was Human-God? Had it no essential sacredness, no *noli-me-tangere* quality of shining away the gambler's covetous glance, of withering his rude and venturous hand, or of poisoning, like some Nessus' shirt, the lewd ruffian who might soon thereafter wear it? Not in the least. This woven web, to which a corrupted state of feeling on religion would have raised cathedrals as its palaces, with singing men and singing women, and singing eunuchs too, to celebrate its virtues; this coarse cloth of some poor weaver's, working down by the sea of Galilee or in some lane of Zion, was still to remain, and be a mere unglorified, economical, useful garment. Far from testifying to its own internal mightiness, it probably was soon sold by the fortunate Roman die-thrower to a second-hand shop of the Jewish metropolis; and so descended from beggar to beggar till it was clean worn out. We never hear that, however easy of access so inestimable relic might then have been considered, any one of the numerous disciples, in the fervour of their earliest zeal, threw away one thought for its redemption. Is it not strange that no St. Helena was at hand to conserve such a desirable invention? Why is there no St. Vestment to keep in countenance a St. Sepulchre and a St. Cross? The poor cloth, in primitive times, really was despised. We know well enough what happened afterwards about handkerchiefs imbued with miraculous properties from holy Paul's body for the nonce: but this is an inferior question, and the matter was temporary; the superior case is proved, and besides the rule *omne majus continet in se minus* there are differences quite intelligible between the cases, whereabout our time would be less profitably employed than in passing on and leaving them unquestioned. Suffice it to say, that "God worked those special miracles," and not the unconscious "handkerchiefs or aprons." "Te Deum laudamus!" is Protestantism's cry; "Sudaria laudemus!" would swell the Papal choirs.

Let such considerations as these then are in sample serve to show how evidently one might prove from anterior circumstances, (and the canon of Scripture is an anterior circumstance,) the probability of the rise and progress of the Roman heresies. And if any one should ask, how was such a system more likely to arise under a Gentile rather than a Jewish theocracy? why was a St. Paul, or a St. Peter, or a St. Dunstan, or a St. Gengulphus, more previously expectable than a St. Abraham, a St. David, a St. Elisha, or a St. Gehazi? I answer, from the idea of idolatry, so adapted to the Gentile mind, and so abhorrent from the Jewish. Martyred Abel, however well respected, has never reached the honours of a niche beside the altar. Jephtha's daughter, for all her mourned virginity, was never paraded, (that I wot of,) for any other than a much-to-be-lamented damsel. Who ever asked, in those old times, the mediation of St. Enoch? Where were the offerings, in jewels or in gold, to propitiate that undoubted man of God and denizen of heaven, St. Moses? what prows, in wax, of vessels saved from shipwreck, hung about the dripping fane of Jonah? and where was, in the olden time, that wretched and insensate being, calling himself rational and godly, who had ventured to solicit the good services of Isaiah as his intercessor, or to plead the merits of St. Ezekiel as the make-weight for his sins?

It was just this, and reasonably to have been expected; for when the Jew brought in his religion, he demolished every false god, broke their images, slew their priests, and burnt their groves with fire. But, when a worldly Christianity came to be in vogue, when emperors adorned their banners with the cross, and the poor fishermen of Galilee, (in their portly representatives,) came to be encrusted with gems, and rustling with seric silk; then was made that fatal compromise; then it was likely to have been made, which has lasted even until now: a compromise which, newly baptizing the damned idols of the heathen, keeps yet St. Bacchus and St. Venus, St. Mars and St. Apollo, perched in sobered robes upon the so-called Christian altar; which yet pays divine honours to an ancyle or a rusty nail; to the black stones at Delphi, or the gold-shrined bones at Aix; which yet sanctifies the chickens of the capitol, or the cock that startled Peter; which yet lets a wealthy sinner, by his gold, bribe the winking Pythoness, or buy dispensing clauses from "the Lord our God, the Pope."

There is yet a swarm of other notions pressing on the mind, which tend to prove that Popery might have been anticipated. Take this view. The religion of Christ is holy, self-denying; not of this world's praise, and ending with the terrible sanction of eternity for good or evil: it sets up God alone supreme, and cuts down creature-merit to a point perpetually diminishing; for the longer he does well, the more he owes to the grace which enabled him to do it.

Now, man's nature is, as we know, diametrically opposite to all this: and unable to escape from the conviction of Christian truth in some sense, he would bend his shrewd invention to the attempt of warping that stern truth to shapes more consistent with his idiosyncrasies. A religious plan might be expected, which, in lieu of a difficult, holy spirituality, should exact easy, mere observances; to say a thousand Paters with the tongue, instead of one "Our Father," from the heart; to exact genuflections by the score, but not a single prostration of the spirit; to write the cross in water on the forehead often-times, but never once to bear its mystic weight upon the shoulder. In spite of self-denial, cleverly kept in sight by means of eggs, and pulse, and hair-cloth, to pamper the deluded flesh with many a carnal holiday; in contravention of a kingdom not of this world, boldly to usurp the temporal dominion of it all: instead of the overwhelming incomprehensibility of an eternal doom, to comfort the worst with false assurance of a purgatory longer or shorter; that after all, vice may be burnt out; and who knows but that gold, buying up the prayers and superfluous righteousness of others, may not make the fiery ordeal an easy one? In lieu of a God brought near to his creatures, infinite purity in contact with the grossest sin, as the good Physician loveth; how sage it seemed to stock the immeasurable distance with intermediate numia, cycle on epicycle, arc on arc, priest and bishop and pope, and martyr, and virgin, and saint, and angel, all in their stations, at due interval soliciting God to be (as if His blessed Majesty were not so of Himself!) the sinner's friend. How comfortable this to man's sweet estimation of his own petty penances; how glorifying to those "filthy rags," his so-called righteousness: how apt to build up the hierarchist power; how seemingly analogous with man's experience here, where clerks lay the case before commissioners, and commissioners before the government, and the government before the sovereign.

All this was entirely expectable: and I can conceive that a deep Reasoner among the first apostles, even without such supernal light as "the Spirit speaking expressly," might have so calculated on the probabilities to come, as to have written, long ago, words akin to these: "In the latter times some shall depart from the faith, giving heed to seductive doctrines, and fanciful notions about intermediate deities, (δαιμονίων,) perverting truth by hypocritical departures from it, searing conscience against its own cravings after spiritual holiness, forbidding marriage, (to invent another virtue,) and commanding abstinence from God's good gifts, as a means of building up a creature-merit by voluntary humiliation." At the likelihood that such "profane and old wives' fables" should thereafter have arisen, might Paul without a miracle have possibly arrived.

Yet again: take another view. The Religion of Christ, though intended to be universal in some better era of this groaning earth, was, until that era cometh, meant and contrived for any thing rather than a Catholicity. True, the Church is so far Catholic that it numbers of its blessed company men of every clime and every age, from righteous Abel down to the last dear babe christened yester-morning; true, the commission is "to all nations, teaching them:" but, what mean the simultaneous and easily reconciled expressions—come out from among them, little flock, gathered out of the Gentiles, a peculiar people, a church militant, and not triumphant, here on earth? Thus shortly of a word much misinterpreted: let us now see what the Romanist does, what, (on human principles,) he would be probable to do, with this discriminating religion. He, chiefly for temporal gains, would make it as expansive as possible: there should be room at that table for every guest, whether wedding-garmented or not; there would be sauces in that poisonous feast, fitted to every palate. For the cold, ascetical mind, a cell and a scourge, and a record kept of starving fancies as calling them ecstatic visions vouchsafed by some old Stylite to bless his favoured worshipper; for the painted demirep of fashionable life, there would be a pretty pocket-idol, and the snug confessional well tenanted by a not unsympathizing father; for the pure girl, blighted in her heart's first love, the papist would afford that seemingly merciful refuge, that calm and musical and gentle place, the irrevocable nunnery; a place, for all its calmness, and its music, and its gentle reputations, soon to be abhorred of that poor child as a living tomb, the extinguisher of all life's aims, all its duties, uses and delights: for the bandit, a tythe of the traveller's gold would avail to pay away the murder, and earn for him a heap of merits kept within the cash-box: the educated, high-born and finely-moulded mind might be well amused with architecture, painting, carving, sweet odours, and the most wondrous music that has ever cheated man, even while he offers up his easy adorations, and departs, equally complacent at the choral remedies as at the priestly absolution; while, for those good few, the truly pious and enlightened children of Rome, who mourn the corruptions of their church, and explain away, with trembling tongue, her obvious errors and idolatries, for these the wily scheme, so probable, devised an undoubted mass of truth to be left among the rubbish. True doctrines, justly held by true martyrs and true saints, holy men of God who have died in that communion; ordinances and an existence which creep up, (heedless of corruption though,) step by step, through past antiquity, to the very feet of the Founder; keen casuists, competent to prove any point of conscience or objection, and that indisputably, for they climax all by the high authority of Popes and councils that cannot be deceived: pious treatises and manuals, verily of flaming heat, for they mingle the yearnings of a constrained celibacy with the fervencies of worship and the cravings after God. Yes, there is meat here for every human mouth; only that, alas for men! the meat is that which perisheth, and not endureth unto everlasting life. Rome, thou wert sagely schemed; and if Lucifer devised thee not for the various appetencies of poor, deceivable, Catholic Man, verily it were pity, for thou art worthy of his handiwork. All things to all men, in any sense but the right, signifies nothing to anybody: in the sense of falsehoods, take the former for thy motto; in that of single truth, in its intensity, the latter.

Let not then the accident—the probable accident—of the Italian superstition place any hindrance in the way of one whose mind is all at sea because of its existence. What, O man with a soul, is all the world else to thee? Christianity, whatever be its broad way of pretences, is but in reality a narrow path: be satisfied with the day of small things, stagger not at the inconsistencies, conflicting words, and hateful strifes of those who say they are Christians, but "are not, but are of the synagogue of Satan." Judge truth, neither by her foes nor by her friends but by herself. There was one who said (and I never heard that any writer, from Julian to Hobbes, ever disputed his human truth or wisdom) "Needs must that offences come; but wo be to that man by whom the offence cometh. If they come, be not shaken in faith: lo, I have told you before. And if others fall away, or do ought else than my bidding, what is that to thee? follow thou ME."

THE BIBLE.

WHILST I attempt to show, as now I desire to do, that the Bible should be just the book it is, from considerations of anterior probability, I must expand the subject a little; dividing it, first, into the likelihood of a revelation at all; and secondly, into that of its expectable form and character.

The first likelihood has its birth in the just Benevolence of our heavenly Father, who without dispute never leaves his rational creatures unaided by some sort of guiding light, some manifestation of himself so needful to their happiness, some sure word of consolation in sorrow, or of brighter hope in persecution. That it must have been thus an *à priori* probability, has been all along proved by the innumerable pretences of the kind so constant up and down the world: no nation ever existed in any age or country, whose seers and wise men of whatever name have not been believed to hold commerce with the Godhead. We may judge from this, how probable it must ever have been held. The Sages of old Greece were sure of it from reason: and not less sure from accepted superstition those who reverenced the Brahmin, or the priest of Heliopolis, or the medicine-man among the Rocky Mountains, or the Llama of old Mexico. I know that our ignorance of some among the most brutalized species of mankind, as the Bushmen in Caffraria, and the tribes of New South Wales, has failed to find among their rites any thing akin to religion: but what may we not yet have to learn of good even about such poor outcasts? how shall we prove this negative? For aught we know, their superstitions at the heart may be as deep and as deceitful as in others; and, even on the contrary side, the exception proves the rule: the rule that every people concluded a revelation so likely, that they have one and all contrived it for themselves.

Thus shortly of the first: and now, secondly, how should God reveal himself to men? In such times as those when the world was yet young, and the Church concentrated in a family or an individual, it would probably be by an immediate oral teaching; the Lord would speak with Adam; He would walk with Enoch; He would, in some pure ethereal garb, talk with Abraham, as friend to friend. And thereafter, as men grew, and worshippers were multiplied, He would give some favoured servant a commission to be His ambassador: He would say to an Ezekiel, "Go unto the house of Israel, and speak my words to them:" He would bid a Jeremiah "Take thee a roll of a book, and write therein all the words that I have spoken to thee:" He would give Daniel a deep vision, not to be interpreted for ages, "Shut up the words, and seal the book even to the time of the end:" He would make

Moses grave His precepts in the rock, and Job record his trials with a pen of iron. For a family, the Beatic Vision was enough: for a congregated nation, as once at Sinai, oral proclamations: for one generation or two around the world, the zeal and eloquence of some great "multitude of preachers:" but, indubitably, if God willed to bless the universal race, and drop the honey of his words distilling down the hour-glass of Time from generation to generation even to the latter days, there was no plan more probable, none more feasible, than the pen of a ready writer.

Further: and which concerns our argument: what were likely to be the characteristic marks of such a revelation? Exclusively of a pervading holiness, and wisdom, and sublimity, which could not be dispensed with, and in some sort should be worthy of the God; there would be, it was probable, frequent evidences of man's infirmity, corrupting all he toucheth. The Almighty works no miracles for little cause: one miracle alone need be current throughout Scripture: to wit, that which preserves it clean and safe from every perilous error. But, in the succession of a thousand scribes each copying from the other, needs must that the tired hand and misty eye would occasionally misplace a letter: this was no nodus worthy of a God's descent to dissipate by miracle.

Again: the original prophets themselves were men of various characters and times and tribes. God addresses men through their reason; he bound not down a seer "with bit and bridle, like the horse that has no understanding"—but spoke as to a rational being—"What seest thou?" "Hear my words;"—"Give ear unto my speech." Was it not then likely that the previous mode of thought and providential education in each holy man of God should mingle irresistibly with his inspired teaching? Should not the herdsman of Tehoa plead in pastoral phrase, and the royal son of Amoz denounce with strong authority? Should not David whilst a shepherd praise God among his flocks, and when a king, cry "Give the King thy judgments?" The Bible is full of this human individuality; and nothing could be thought as humanly more probable: but we must, with this diversity, connect the other probability also, that which should show the work to be divine; which would prove (as is literally the case) that, in spite of all such natural variety, all such unbiassed freedom both of thought and speech, there pervades the whole mass a oneness, a marvellous consistency, which would be likely to have been designed by God, though little to have been dreamt by man.

Once more on this full topic. Difficulties in Scripture were expectable for many reasons; I can only touch a few. Man is rational as he is responsible: God speaks to his mind and moral powers: and the mind rejoices, and moralities grow strong in conquest of the difficult and search for the mysterious. The muscles of the spiritual athlete pant for such exertion; and without it, they would dwindle into trepid imbecility. Curious man, courageous man, enterprising, shrewd, and vigourous man, yet has a constant enemy to dread in his own indolence: now, a lion in the path will wake up Sloth himself: and the very difficulties of religion engender perseverance.

Additionally: I think there is somewhat in the consideration, that, if all revealed truth had been utterly simple and easy, it would have needed no human interpreter; no enlightened class of men, who, according to the spirit of their times, and the occasions of their teaching, might "in season and out of season preach the word, reprove, rebuke, exhort, with all long-suffering and doctrine." I think there existed an anterior probability that Scripture should be as it is, often-times difficult, obscure, and requiring the aid of many wise to its elucidation; because, without such characteristic, those many wise and good would never have been called for. Suppose all truth revealed as clearly and indisputably to the meanest intellect as a sum in addition is, where were the need or use of that noble Christian company who are every where man's almoners for charity, and God's ambassadors for peace?

A word or two more, and I have done. The Bible would, as it seems to me probable, be a sort of double book; for the righteous, and for the wicked: to one class, a decoy, baited to allure all sorts of generous dispositions: to the other, a trap, set to catch all kinds of evil inclinations. In these two senses, it would address the whole family man: and every one should find in it something to his liking. Purity should there perceive green pastures and still waters, and a tender Shepherd for its innocent steps: and carnal appetite should here and there discover some darker spot, which the honesty of heaven had filled with memories of its chiefest servants' sins; some record of adultery or murder wherewith to feast his maw for condemnation. While the good man should find in it meat divine for every earthly need, the sneerer should proclaim it the very easiest manual for his jests and lewd profanities. The unlettered should not lack humble, nay vulgar, images and words, to keep himself in countenance: neither should the learned look in vain for reasonings; the poet for sublimities; the curious mind for mystery; nor the sorrowing heart for prayer. I do discern, in that great book, a wondrous adaptability to minds of every calibre: and it is just what might antecedently have been expected of a volume writ by many men at many different eras, yet all superintended by one master mind; of a volume meant for every age, and nation, and country, and tongue, and people; of a volume which, as a two-edged sword, wounds the good man's heart with deep conviction, and cuts down "the hoary head of him who goeth on still in his wickedness."

On the whole, respecting faults, or incongruities, or objectionable parts in Scripture, however to have been expected, we must recollect that the more they are viewed, the more the blemishes fade, and are altered into beauties.

A little child had picked up an old stone, defaced with time-stains: the child said the stone was dirty, covered with blotches and all colours: but his father brings a microscope, and shows to his astonished glance that what the child thought dirt, is a forest of beautiful lichens, fruited mosses, and strange lilliputian plants with shapely animalcules hiding in the leaves, and rejoicing in their tiny shadow. Every blemish, justly seen, had turned to be a beauty: and Nature's works are vindicated good, even as the Word of Grace is wise.

HEAVEN AND HELL.

PROBABLY enough, the light which I expect to throw upon this important subject will, upon a cursory criticism, be judged fanciful, erroneous, and absurd; in parts, quite open to ridicule, and in all liable to the objection of being wise, or foolish, beyond what is written. Nevertheless, and as it seems to me of no small consequence to reach something more definite on the subject than the Anywhere or Nowhere of common apprehensions, I judge it not amiss to put out a few thoughts, fancies, if you will, but not unreasonable fancies, on the localities and other characteristics of what we call heaven and hell: in fact, I wish to show their probable realities with somewhat approaching to distinctness. It is manifest that these places must be somewhere; for, more especially of the blest estate, whither did Enoch, and Elijah, and our risen Lord ascend to? what became of these glorified humanities when "the chariot of fire carried up Elijah by a whirlwind into heaven;" and when "HE was taken up, and a cloud received him?" Those happy mortals did not waste away to intangible spiritualities, as they rose above the world; their bodies were not melted as they broke the bonds of gravitation, and pierced earth's swathing atmosphere: they went up somewhither; the question is where they went to. It is a question of great interest to us; however, among those matters which are rather curious than consequential; for in our own case, as we know, we that are redeemed are to be caught up, together with other blessed creatures, "in the clouds, to meet our coming Saviour in the air, and thereafter to be ever with the Lord." I wish to show this to be expected as in our case, and expectable previously to it.

We have, in the book of Job, a peep at some place of congregation: some one, as it is likely, of the mighty globes in space, set apart as God's especial temple. Why not? they all are worlds; and the likelihood being in favour of overbalancing good, rather than of preponderating evil from considerations that affect God's attributes and the happiness of his creatures, it is probable that the great majority of these worlds are unfallen mansions of the blessed. Perhaps each will be a kingdom for one of earth's redeemed, and if so, there will at last be found fulfilled that prevailing superstition of our race, that each man has his star: without insisting upon this, we may reflect that there is no one universal opinion which has not its foundation in truth. Tradition may well have dropped the thought from Adam downwards, that the stars may some day be our thrones. We know their several vastness, and can guess their glory: verily a mighty meed for miserable services on earth, to find a just ambition gladdened with the rule of spheres, to which Terra is a point; while that same ambition is sanctified and legalized by ruling as vicegerent of Jehovah.

Is this unlikely, or unworthy of our high vocation, our immortality, and nearness unto, nay communion with God? The idea is only suggested: let a man muse at midnight, and look up at the heavens hanging over all; let him see, with Rosse and Herschell, that, multiply power as you will, unexhausted still and inexhaustible appear the myriads of worlds unknown. Yea, there is space enow for infinite reward; yea, let every grain of sand on every shore be gathered, and more innumerable yet appear that galaxy of spheres. Let us think that night looks down upon us here, with the million eyes of heaven. And for some focus of them all, some spot where God himself enthroned receives the homage of all crowns, and the worship of all creature service, what is there unreasonable in suggesting for a place some such an one as is instanced below?

I have just cut the following paragraph out of a newspaper: Is this the ridiculous tripping up the sublime? I think otherwise: it is honest to use plain terms. I speak as unto wise men—judge ye what I say. With respect to the fact of information, it may or it may not be true; but even if untrue, the idea is substantially the same, and I cannot help supposing that with angels and archangels and the whole company of heaven, such bodily saints as Enoch is, (and similar to him all risen, holy men will be,) meet for happy sabbaths in some glorious orb akin or superior to the following:

"A CENTRAL SUN.—Dr. Madier, the Professor of Astronomy at Dorpat, has published the results of the researches pursued by him uninterruptedly during the last sixty years, upon the movements of the so-called fixed stars. These more particularly relate to the star Alcyone, (discovered by him,) the brightest of the seven bright stars of the group of the Pleiades. This star he states to be the central sun of all the systems of stars known to us. He gives its distance from the boundaries of our system at thirty-four million times the distance of the sun from our earth, a distance which it takes five hundred and thirty-seven years for light to traverse. Our sun takes one hundred and eighty-two million years to accomplish its course round this central body, whose mass is one hundred and seventeen million times larger than the sun."

One hundred and seventeen million times larger than the Sun! itself, for all its vastness, not more than half one million times bigger than this earth. To some such globe we may let our fancies float, and anchor there our yearnings after heaven. It is a glorious thought, such as imagination loves; and a probable thought, that commends itself to reason. Behold the great eye of all our guessed creation, the focus of its brightness, and the fountain of its peace.

A topic far less pleasant, but alike of interest to us poor men, is the probable home of evil; and here I may be laughed at—laugh, but listen, and if, listening, some reason meets thine ear, laugh at least no longer.

We know that, for spirit's misery as for spirit's happiness, there is no need of place: "no matter where, for I am still the same," said one most miserable being. More—in the case of mere spirits, there is no need for any apparatus of torments, or fires, or other fearful things. But, when spirit is married to matter, the case is altered; needs must a place to prison the matter, and a corporal punishment to vex it.

Nothing is unlikely here; excepting—will a man urge?—the dread duration of such hell. This is a parenthesis; but it shall not be avoided, for the import of that question is deep, and should be answered clearly. A man, a body and soul inmixt, body risen incorruptible, and soul rested from its deeds, must exist for ever. I touch not here the proofs—assume it. Now, if he lives for ever, and deliberately chooses evil, his will consenting as well as his infirmity, and conscience seared by persisted disobedience, what course can such a wilful, rational, responsible being pursue than one perpetually erratic? How should it not be that he gets worse and worse in morals, and more and more miserable in fact? and when to this we add, that such wretched creatures are to herd together, continually flying further away from the only source of Happiness and Good; and to this, that they have earned by sin, remorses and regrets, and positive inflictions; how probable seems a hell, the sinner's doom eternal. The apt mathematical analogy of lines thrown out of parallel, helps this for illustration: for ever and for ever they are stretching more remote, and infinity itself cannot reünite their travel.

This, then, as a passing word; a sad one. Honest thinker, do not scorn it, for thine own soul's sake. "Now is the time of grace, now is the day of salvation." To return. A place of punishment exists; to what quarter shall we look for its anterior probability? I think there is a likelihood very near us. There may be one, possibly, beneath us, in the bowels of this fiery-bursting earth; whither went Korah and his company? This idea is not without its arguments, just analogies, and scriptural hints. But my judgment inclines towards another. This trial-world, we know, is to be purified and restored, and made a new earth: it was even to be expected that Redemption should do this, and I like not to imagine it the crust and case of hell, but rather, as thus: At the birth of this same world, there was struck off from its burning mass at a tangent, a mournful satellite, to be the home of its immortal evil; the convict shore for exiled sin and misery; a satellite of strange differences, as guessed by Virgil in his musings upon Tartarus, where half the orb is, from natural necessities, blistered up by constant heats, the other half frozen by perennial cold. A land of caverns, and volcanoes, miles deep, miles high; with no water, no perceptible air: imagine such a dreadful world, with neither air nor water! incapable of feeding life like ours, but competent to be a place where undying wretchedness may struggle for ever. A melancholy orb, the queen of night, chief nucleus of all the dark idolatries of earth; the Moon, Isis, Hecate, Ashtaroth, Diana of the Ephesians!

This expression of a thought by no means improbable, gives an easy chance to shallow punsters; but ridicule is no weapon against reason. Why should not the case be so? Why should not Earth's own satellite, void, as yet, be on the resurrection of all flesh, the raft whereon to float away Earth's evil? Read of it astronomically; think of it as connected with idols; regard it as the ruler of earth's night; consider that the place of a Gehenna must be somewhere; and what is there in my fancy quite improbable? I do not dogmatize as that the fact is so, but only suggest a definite place at least as likely as any other hitherto suggested. Think how that awful, melancholy eye looks down on deeds of darkness how many midnight crimes, murders, thefts, adulteries, and witchcrafts, that would have shrunk into nonentity from open, honest day, have paled the conscious Moon! Add to all this, it is the only world, besides our own, whereof astronomers can tell us, It is fallen.

AN OFFER.

NOTHING were easier than to have made this book a long one; but that was not the writer's object: as well because of the musty Greek proverb about long books; which in every time and country are sure never to be read through by one in a thousand; as because it is always wiser to suggest than to exhaust a topic; which may be as "a fruit-tree yielding fruit after its kind whose seed is in itself." The writer then intended only to touch upon a few salient points, and not to discuss every question, however they might crowd upon his mind: time and space alike with mental capabilities forbade an effort so gigantic: added to which, such a course seemed to be unnecessary, as the rule of probability, thus illustrated, might be applied by others in every similar instance. Still, as the errand of this book is usefulness, and its author's hope is, under Heaven, to do good, one personal hint shall here be thrown upon the highway. Without arrogating to myself the wisdom or the knowledge to solve one in twenty of the doubts possible to be propounded; without also designing even to attempt such solutions, unless well assured of the genuine anxiety of the doubter; and preliminarizing the consideration, that a fitting diffidence in the advocate's own powers is no reason why he should not make wide efforts in his holy cause; that, such reasonable essays to do good have no sort of brotherhood with a fanatical Spiritual Quixotism; and that, to my own apprehensions, the doubts of a rationalizing mind are in the nature of honourable foes, to be treated with delicacy, reverence, and kindness, rather than with a cold distance and an ill-concealed contempt; preliminarizing, lastly, the thought—"Who is sufficient for these things?"—I nevertheless thus offer, according to the grace and power given to me, my best but humble efforts so far to dissipate the doubts of some respecting any scriptural fact, as may lie within the province of showing or attempting to show its previous credibility. This is not a challenge to the curious casuist or the sneering infidel; but an invitation to the honest mind harassed by unanswered queries: no gauntlet thrown down, but a brother's hand stretched out. Such questions, if put to the writer, through his publisher by letter, may find their reply in a future edition: supposing, that is to say, that they deserve an answer, whether as regards their own merits or the temper of the mind who doubts; and supposing also that the writer has the power and means to answer them discreetly. It is only a fair rule of philanthropy (and that without arrogating any unusual "strength") to "bear the infirmities of the weak, and not to please ourselves:" and nothing would to me give greater happiness than to be able, as I am willing, to remove any difficulties lying in the track of Faith before a generous mind. I hang out no glistening hollybush a-flame with its ostentatious berries as promising good wine; but rather over my portal is the humbler and hospitable mistletoe, assuring every wearied pilgrim in the way, that though scanty be the fare, he shall find a hearty welcome.

CONCLUSION.

I HAVE thus endeavoured (with solicited help of Heaven) to place before the world anew a few old truths: truths inestimably precious. Remember, they cannot have lost by any such advocacy as is contained in the idea of their being shown antecedently probable; for this idea affects not at all the fact of their existence; the thing is; whether probable or not; there is, in esse, an ornithorhyncus; its posse is drowned in esse: there exists no doubt of it: evidence, whether of senses physical, or of considerations moral, puts the circumstance beyond the sphere of disputation. But such truths as we have spoken of do, nevertheless, gain something as to—not their merits, these are all their own substantially; nor their positive proofs, these are adjectives properly attendant on them, but as to—their acceptability among the incredulous of men; they gain, I say, even by such poor pleading as mine, from being shown anteriorly probable. Take an illustration in the case of that strange and anomalous creature mentioned just above. Its habitat is in a land where plums grow with the stones outside, where aboriginal dogs have never been heard to bark, where birds are found covered with hair, and where mammals jump about like frogs! If these are shown to be literal facts, the mind is thereby well prepared for any animal monstrosity: and it staggers not in unbelief (on evidence of honest travellers) even when informed of a creature with a duck's bill and a beaver's body: it really amounted in Australia to an antecedent probability.

Carry this out to matters not a quarter so incredible, ye thinkers, ye free-thinkers; neither be abashed at being named as thinking freely: were not those Bereans more noble in that they searched to see? For my humble part, I do commend you for it: treacherous is the hand that roots up the inalienable right of private judgment; the foundation-stone of Protestantism, the great prerogative of reason, the key-note of conscience, the sole vindex of a man's responsibility: evil and false is the so-called reverential wisdom which lays down in place of the truth that each man's conscience is a law unto himself, the tyranny of other men's authority. Cheap and easy and perilled is the faith, which clings to the skirt of others; which leans upon the broken staff of priestcraft, until those poisoned splinters pierce the hand.

Prove all things; holding fast that which is good: good to thine own reasonable conscience, if unwarped by casuistries, and unblinded by licentiousness. Prove all things, if you can, "from the egg to the apple:" he is a poor builder of his creed, who takes one brick on credit. Be able, as you can be, (if only you are willing so far to be wisely inconsistent, as to bend the stubborn knee betimes, and though with feeble glance to look to heaven, and though with stammering tongue to pray for aid,) be able, as it is thy right, O man of God—to give a Reason for the faith that is in thee.

THE END.